Easy Accounting

Easy Accounting

SIMPLE STEPS, SIMPLE SOLUTIONS

Becky Egan

Title: Easy Accounting - Simple Steps, Simple Solutions
Cover and Interior Layout: Pickawoowoo Publishing Group
Edited: Eddie Elbrecht - Pickawoowoo Publishing Group
Printing & Distribution: Ingram (USA, UK, AUS, EUR)

First Street Press LLC
978-0-578-93288-0 (paperback)
978-0-578-93283-4 (hardback)

First Printing, 2021

For my Dad, Gerry Noack,
who never stopped asking how this book was going.

Contents

INTRODUCTION

Why are You Doing This?

Hello and welcome to *Easy Accounting: Simple Steps, Simple Solutions*. If you are starting a small business, you already have one, or if you're considering going freelance and the idea of keeping track of everything scares you, you've come to the right place. If you're a student of accounting – or you are mystified by accounting and just want to learn more about accounting from someone who does this for a living and can explain it in plain English – you've also come to the right place.

My name is Becky Egan, and I'm a CPA with a tax practice in Manhattan. This means I like numbers and I like accounting – but I also have a teaching mindset so I like to explain accounting to anyone who will listen. My firm works with hundreds of small businesses and freelancers every year to prepare their taxes, and we also help them organize their finances. We work with countless folks each year who are very successful in their own industry but who come into the office saying that they don't 'get' money, or that they're 'not good at' finances. I'm here to tell you that everyone – and I mean everyone – I've worked with can be taught to understand accounting. I've trained hundreds of folks on QuickBooks – my preferred method of accounting recordkeeping – and I haven't had a single failure yet.

Why do you want to have a good accounting system in place? I start every training session with a new client by reminding folks that you have two reasons for doing your bookkeeping. The first is what most folks think of first, and it's actually the least important – for taxes. Yes, I'm a CPA in tax practice, and yes, my firm files thousands of returns each year, so I'm constantly thinking about taxes. But even I realize that it's pretty complex to set up a bookkeeping system just for tax purposes. Don't get me wrong, I love when my clients have accurate financials all ready for me at tax time – makes my job much easier. But the number one most important reason to do your books is for yourself and your business. You want to see where the money is coming from, when it's coming in, how much you spend each month and why, and what your profit is. That is the most important reason to do your books – so you can unlock valuable data to help you make decisions about your business.

Also, and this is a lesser-known benefit to accounting, when you keep a set of books, everything gets entered in two places. This is called double-entry bookkeeping, and we'll get to the specifics of it later. But for now, realize that when your books are balanced, every debit matches a credit, the Assets equal the Liabilities and Equity, and there is a harmony in the universe. How many other areas in your life tie out this neatly? Very few, I'd wager. There is something amazingly satisfying and therapeutic about the accounting process.

This book is different from a traditional accounting book – and not only because I've just posited that accounting has mental health benefits! I wrote this book after giving countless QuickBooks training sessions to my clients over the past 10-plus years. In each session, in order to train my client in how to use QuickBooks, I have always spent time explaining the general principles of accounting first – and then expanding on those principles during the lesson. I realized after giving so many lessons on accounting basics that I'd developed an easy-to-understand way to walk folks through the basic tenets of accounting. And because accounting is something I love so much but which is often confusing to people, I wrote this book to share my passion for accounting by explaining it in an easy-to-understand way.

The book opens with the very basics in Part One where we'll tackle the basic financial statements, the chart of accounts, debits and credits, journal entries, T-accounts, and more. If what I've just written sounds like a foreign language, don't worry, we'll go through these concepts in detail with lots of examples while we go.

Part Two gets into more advanced accounting topics – cash versus accrual, depreciation, inventory and more. These are topics that include words you'll hear about often, and they will no longer be mysterious.

At the end of both Part One and Part Two, you'll have some exercises you can try on your own to see if you've gotten the hang of it. It's vital that you really do these! Going through the process of making journal entries, posting to the T-accounts and preparing the financial statements is how you'll cement this knowledge into your brain, and you'll have a deeper understanding of the concepts you have read about.

So, as I tell my clients when I send them off to do QuickBooks homework, pour a glass of wine, get comfy and get ready for some easy accounting!

Part One

Easy Accounting Basics

CHAPTER 1

The Big Two Financial Statements

Whenever I begin explaining accounting to people, I like to begin with the end in mind – the financial statements! For business owners, investors and tax preparers, we need financial statements in order to evaluate our businesses, to evaluate the viability of investing in another business and to prepare our tax returns. Financial statements are reports, and they are produced by summing up all the various transactions that happened over a period of time.

The two big financial statements we're going to focus on here are:

- The Balance Sheet (aka the Statement of Financial Position) and
- The Income Statement (aka the Profit and Loss Statement)

These two statements are both critical, and they tie together in a very neat way.

The Balance Sheet

What is a Balance Sheet? Also known as a statement of financial position, it shows what you OWN, minus what you OWE, and the RESULT is your Equity. It's important to note that the balance sheet is a snapshot, not a filmstrip. This means that the balance sheet shows where you are at a specific moment in time – nothing more. Your balance sheet could change dramatically the day after you prepare it. Keep this in mind as you review balance sheets from other companies as well.

When you look at a balance sheet, you'll notice there are three components:

1) What you OWN – These are your Assets. For many businesses, which are consulting or service businesses, this is your cash. These businesses don't require fancy equipment as they are likely selling their time or expertise. For businesses that sell stuff, or make stuff, their assets will be a little more complex – cash, equipment, tools, buildings, vehicles, inventory, etc.

Your assets are expected to bring you income in the future – inventory can be sold for cash, and equipment helps you make inventory that can be sold; you will eventually leave your leased retail space and get that security deposit back. Assets are listed on the balance sheet in order of liquidity. Liquidity is a fancy word for how quickly something can be turned into cash. So, the first item on all balance sheets is always Cash or Checking. The least liquid item is usually a building or land because it's very hard, time-consuming and expensive to sell a building and receive cash for it.

2) What you OWE – These are your Liabilities. For many small businesses, this is a credit card. This could also be a bank loan or line of credit, or a loan to the business from a shareholder or a family member. For bigger companies this is bonds or notes.

Your liabilities are a drain on cash flow – you typically have to make payments on these on a regular basis, or maybe you will have to pay these off over time. Just as with assets, liabilities are presented on the balance sheet in order of their due dates, so a credit card would be listed before a mortgage.

3) Your Equity is the RESULT. Equity confuses people but it doesn't have to. There are two ways to think about equity – it's either what you'd have left if you sold off all your assets to pay off all your liabilities (because Assets minus Liabilities equals Equity – this is the Basic Accounting Equation and we'll come back to it later) or it's the netting out of all the money you put into the company and all the money you've taken out and the profit or loss over time.

Just like the Assets of a business are made up of many accounts (i.e., cash, inventory), the Equity of a business is also made up of many accounts. For small businesses, this is usually something like:

- Owner Contributions – money the owner put into the business. These increase your total equity.
- Owner Distributions – money the owner took out of the business. These decrease the total equity.

- Net Income – the current-year profit of the business. More on that later.
- Retained Earnings – the cumulative profit of the business over its lifetime.

Note that in large companies (i.e., publicly traded corporations) equity would also include stock. This is a direct investment into a company from investors. Stock investment is important when looking at large companies' books or when evaluating a potential investment, but for our purposes here – small business accounting – we are going to stick with the categories above.

To illustrate the balance sheet, let's do a quick example.

(1) You start a consulting business. To do so, you put $100 of your own money into your newly opened business bank account. You now have Assets of $100 (Checking) and Equity of $100 (Owner's Contributions).

Recall here that I said you need to enter everything you do in *two places* (double entry bookkeeping) – thus, when you invest money into your business, you don't just add the $100 to the checking account and call it a day. You also need to say where it *came from* – was it a loan? Income? Sale of something? No, in this case, it came from your (the owner's) pocket, so, Owner Contributions.

Now, say you want more money in the bank and (2) take out a loan of $400 from your cousin (this is not advisable, by the way). Now you have $500 in the bank (Checking – Asset), a loan of $400 (Family Loan Payable – Liability) and equity of $100 (Owner's Contribution – Equity).

Do you see that if you paid off your liabilities of $400, you'd have $100 left, which is equal to your equity? This is like the beautiful algebraic property, the Additive Property of Equality, which states that when you add something to both sides of an equation, it still balances.

Look at the equations below that are based on the scenarios above. In (1), you invest your own funds into the bank. In (2), you borrow money to put into the bank.

(1) $100 = $100

   $100 in the bank, $100 in equity

   Assets = (Liabilities – we have none here) + Equity

(2) $100 + $400 = $100 + $400

   Cash you had before + cash you borrowed = money you put in + money you borrowed

$500 in the bank = $400 in liabilities + $100 equity
Assets = Liabilities + Equity
OR
Assets minus Liabilities = Equity

These equations are equivalent.

Here is what that second scenario, of adding your own money and borrowing some money, would look like, translated into a formal balance sheet.

<table>
<tr><td colspan="4" align="center">My Consulting Business
Balance Sheet
As of June 30, 20xx</td></tr>
<tr><td>ASSETS</td><td></td><td>LIABILITIES</td><td></td></tr>
<tr><td>Checking</td><td>$500</td><td>Family Loan Payable</td><td>$400</td></tr>
<tr><td>Total Assets</td><td><u>$500</u></td><td>Total Liabilities</td><td><u>$400</u></td></tr>
<tr><td></td><td></td><td>EQUITY</td><td></td></tr>
<tr><td></td><td></td><td>Owner's Contributions</td><td>$100</td></tr>
<tr><td></td><td></td><td>Total Equity</td><td><u>$100</u></td></tr>
<tr><td></td><td></td><td>Total Liabilities & Equity</td><td><u>$500</u></td></tr>
</table>

Notice that for a balance sheet, we always show three things in the title: the name of the Company, the type of financial statement (Balance Sheet), and the 'as of' date. Recall that above I mentioned the balance sheet is a snapshot, thus the date is 'as of', not for a period, like a year, a month, or a week. This is because a balance sheet shows the financial position of a company at a certain point in time. Accountants call the balance sheet a snapshot, because it literally freezes the financial position of a company at a certain point in time. The very next day the balance sheet could look totally different but at the point in time in which it's stated, it shows the company's financial position.

Also note this balance sheet graphically depicts what I referred to earlier as the Basic Accounting Equation:

Assets = Liabilities + Equity

By showing the assets on the left side and the liabilities and equity on the right side, we basically impute a large "equals sign" down the middle of the page. And you'll notice, again, that the assets do indeed equal the liabilities plus the equity.

Balance sheets are not always presented this way, with assets on the left and liabilities and equity on the right. Sometimes they are given vertically down the pages, with assets first, then liabilities and then equity. But I like presenting balance sheets this way because it so very clearly shows the Basic Accounting Equation.

The Income Statement

Let's now talk about the Income Statement. This is also called the Profit & Loss Statement, meaning, at the end of the statement you get down to a profit (we hope) or a loss (we hope not). This is made up of INCOME and EXPENSES, and I often find that for my clients, this statement is the easier one to wrap their minds around. It's also known as the results of operations. At the end of the day, how much money did you make?

An important note here – there are two ways to run your income statement: cash-basis accounting, and accrual-basis accounting. We'll get into this in Chapter Four. For now, because cash-basis accounting is much, much simpler, and it's what the vast majority of small businesses use, we're going to stick with this.

INCOME is what you get for selling something – your time or a product (whether a physical product or a service). Most businesses use several income accounts to keep track of their sales – e.g., Consulting Income, Referral Income, Sales of Product A, Sales of Product B, etc.

EXPENSES are costs incurred to help you run your business. Most businesses have many accounts they use to track their expenses – Rent expense, Office supplies, Salaries, Payroll taxes, etc.

PROFIT or LOSS is simply Income minus Expenses. There is another important type of account that belongs on your balance sheet, something we call a mezzanine account, one that goes in between Income and Expenses. This account is Cost of Goods Sold. We'll get to it in Chapter Six.

Let's go back to our hypothetical consulting business. You make your first sale and get someone to pay you $1000 for a day's worth of consulting (great work, by the way). You had to buy $200 worth of office supplies so you can write your report to the client, though. Your profit, then, is $800, because Income ($1000) minus Expenses ($200) equals your Profit ($800).

Translated into an Income Statement, we have:

My Consulting Business
Income Statement
For the Period June 30, 20xx

INCOME		
Consulting Sales	$1000	
Total Income		$1000
EXPENSES		
Office Supplies	($200)	
Total Expenses		($200)
NET PROFIT		$800

Note that we total the income and expenses separately, usually in their own column, and then we subtract the expenses from the income to get to Profit. This graphically depicts the subtraction that we do – income minus expenses equals profit.

It's also convention to have the expenses written in red or placed in parentheses. The same convention goes for a negative number, so if you have a net loss instead of net profit, you'd use parentheses to show that negative number.

Also note that for income statements, similarly to balance sheets, we always show three things in the title: the name of the company, the type of financial statement (Income Statement), and the 'for the period' dates, because again, income statements are for a period of time, a filmstrip. Again, this differs from the format of the date for the Balance Sheet. The Balance Sheet reflects a point in time. But the Income Statement shows amounts earned and spent during a certain period. In this example, it's the results of operations for one day, June 30, 20xx. But you can have an income statement for a week, a month, a quarter, a year – any period of time.

Finally, note that in the first example, where you funded your account and then borrowed money to add to what was in the bank, you had no income and no expenses, and thus nothing showed up on your income statement. Equity contributions and taking out a loan are solely Balance Sheet items and do not show up on the income statement. Moving money from one asset account to another, or using assets to pay off liabilities, or taking equity withdrawals out of assets are all what we call balance sheet transfers. Everything that changed happens within accounts that live on the balance sheet only. But how do we know which accounts live on the balance sheet, and which live on the income statement? This leads into our next topic, which is your Chart of Accounts.

CHAPTER 2

Chart of Accounts, and What in the World are Debits and Credits

Now that we understand the two big financial statements used in accounting, we can turn to the accounts that make up those statements. We've already named a few accounts in explaining the financial statements – Checking, Family Loan Payable, Consulting Revenue, Owner's Contribution. You'll see these all explained in more detail below, and you'll also see where they end up on the financial statements.

The Chart of Accounts

Every business has what is called a Chart of Accounts, which is just a listing of all the accounts used in the business. Every account belongs *either* on the Balance Sheet or the Income Statement but *not* both. This is an important and often overlooked point.

Recall in our prior example that you made an Owner's Contribution of $100 to your business and put that money into the bank. Then you also borrowed $400 from a family member and also put that into the bank. The accounts in question here are:

- Owner's Contribution (Equity)
- Family Loan (Liability)
- Checking/Cash (Asset)

All of these are balance sheet accounts, which means they belong on the balance sheet. Recall too that none of those transactions had anything to do with income, so there would be no effect on the income statement for those transactions.

Similarly, we talked about income statement accounts in the example where you earned some consulting revenue and bought office supplies. The accounts in question here are:

- Consulting Revenue (Income)
- Office Supplies (Expenses)

However, in that example we didn't include *all* the accounts that were affected. If you earned $1000 of consulting revenue, where did that money go? To the bank, of course! And how did you buy the office supplies? With cash, a check, or a debit card. So, we didn't tell the whole story in that example yet, but we're going to now.

Debits and Credits

Everything that happens in a business can be put into the bookkeeping world through a few simple steps:

1. Make a journal entry (more on this in a moment)
2. Post to a T-account (more on these in a moment)
3. Then eventually close out the books to the financial statements (which you learned about in Chapter One)

In order to talk about these, we first need to talk about debits and credits.

But in order to do that, we first need to talk about T-accounts.

Back in the pre-QuickBooks and accounting software days, accountants and bookkeepers used to keep track of their books in the general ledger – a really big book with a lot of pages. Every account in the Chart of Accounts (just a big list) had a T-account where each transaction was posted. T-accounts are old-fashioned, yes, and you will not need to use them when you keep your own books anymore – software can do that. But learning how to use these is the absolute best way to help understand the accounting process.

Here is what those T-accounts look like:

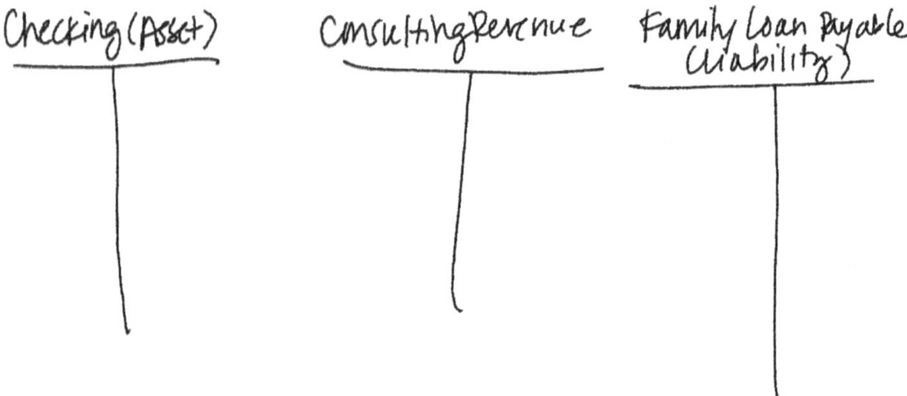

They're called T-accounts because they look like the letter T – a line down the middle and space to the left of the line and space to the right of the line.

Do these look somewhat familiar? Maybe? A T-account, with a line down the middle, is similar to the balance sheet as I presented it in the prior chapter. Assets were on the left, and liabilities and equity were on the right.

You can make a debit or a credit entry to every single type of account. The effect it has on the account, whether it increases it or decreases it, depends on the type of account it is.

But the really super easy thing about debits and credits is this – if you want to debit an account, you put that number on the left side of the T-account. To credit the account, put it on the right. Remember:

- Debits on the left
- Credits on the right

In accounting, that is all the words 'debit' and 'credit' mean: debit = left, credit = right.

Depending on what type of account you're working with, a debit will either increase or decrease your total.

Here is the reference point for this:

	Balance Sheet Accounts			Income Statement Accounts	
	Assets	Liabilities	Equity	Revenue	Expense
Debit	+	—	—	—	+
Credit	—	+	+	+	—

So, according to the chart above:

- To increase an asset, you debit it. To decrease, credit it.
- To increase a liability, you credit it. To decrease, debit it.
- To increase your equity, you credit it. To decrease, debit it.
- To increase a revenue, you credit it. To decrease, debit it.
- To increase an expense, you debit it. To decrease, credit it.

If this all seems confusing, hang in there for a few more moments as it's about to become clearer. Let's go through the steps of bookkeeping one by one.

The Accounting Cycle, Simplified

Recall that we said the steps in bookkeeping were:

1. Make a journal entry
2. Post to a T-account
3. Then eventually close out the books to the financial statements

Let's look at step one.

1) Journal Entries

In the old, pre-computer days, the general journal is where all business transactions were recorded. A journal entry, then, is how you record specific business events. Each journal entry has four parts:

1. The date
2. One or more debits
3. One or more credits
4. A description of the event

Going back to our good old example from Chapter One, you start your consulting business and fund the bank account with $100 of your own money. Here is the journal entry for that transaction.

June 30, 20xx
DR Checking (asset) $100
 CR Owner's Contributions (equity) $100
To record owner's initial contribution to bank account.

Note we have a date, because we need to know when this happened so we can put in the right period when we post to the financials. We also use the abbreviations DR for debit and CR for credit. Typically, we indent slightly when we get to the CR portion of the entry. Finally, we use words to tell what happened. This is not so important in this case, as we can pretty much figure out what happened, but it is good to get into the habit of putting a quick explanation after all entries you use.

You'll see too that eventually we can have more than one debit and more than one credit in any given entry. We'll get to examples of that in later chapters.

Finally, note that in this entry the debits equal the credits. This always has to be the case. In order for the whole system to work:

The debits must always equal the credits.

This is the crux of double-entry bookkeeping, and it's the crux of keeping the accounting universe in balance. Remembering this maxim will really help you if you ever get to a business transaction that you can't figure out – just begin the process of creating a journal entry. If you get to a place where you have more debits than credits, you know you need to add a credit to get it to balance. Similarly, if you have more credits than debits, you need to add a debit to get it to balance. It's a useful tool in making sense of any transaction you encounter.

2) Post to T-Accounts

After you make the journal entry in the general journal, you would then in the old days post those to the respective T-accounts in the general ledger. So, every account that is included in that journal entry would have its entry posted to its T-account. Thus, back to our first journal entry, your T-accounts would look like this:

Checking	Owner's Equity
100	100

As you can see, to increase the asset account, we debited it. Then to increase the Owner's Contributions account, we credited it. Check back to the reference point on page 13 to refresh your memory. Trust me, before long this will be second nature and you won't need the reference anymore.

Now let's make the journal entry for the loan you took from your cousin.

June 30, 20xx
DR Checking (asset) $400
 CR Family Loan Payable (liabilities) $400
To record loan received from family member.

Notice that even though we know from our previous work that the TOTAL in the bank now is $500, you just debit his particular example by the $400 you've just received from the loan. Thus, the debits equal the credits.

Then, when we post these to the T-accounts, we get:

Checking	Family loan	Owner's Equity
100	400	100
400		
500		

Thus, our balance in the checking account is the sum of the $100 you invested plus the $400 from your loan, or $500. You can total these here simply by adding, because they are both debits to an asset account. You would need to subtract or net if you have entries on both sides of the T-bar because one side represents an increase, while the other side represents a decrease.

Now, let's do the two journal entries we did in the examples to get the income statement going. Once we 'journalize' them, or make the entries, we can then post to the T-accounts and go back to the financial statements to bring it all full circle.

Recall that you earned and received $1000 in consulting revenue and you spent $200 on office supplies.

Let's assume that you received a check for this revenue and you deposited it into your business checking account.

June 30, 20xx
DR Checking $1000
 CR Consulting Revenue $1000
To record revenue earned and received from Client A.

Notice that this is the first entry we've made so far that includes accounts from BOTH the balance sheet and the income statement. The Checking account is an asset and lives on the balance sheet. The Consulting Revenue account is an income account and lives on the income statement.

Next, you bought some office supplies, and for now, let's say you bought them with your debit card linked with your checking account.

June 30, 20xx
DR Office Supplies $200
 CR Checking $200
To record office supplies purchased via checking.

Again, this entry spans both the BS and IS.

So, let's post both of these to our T-accounts.

Checking	Family loan	Owner's Equity
100		400
400		100
500	
1000	200
1300	

Consulting Revenue	Office Supplies
1000	200

Notice that in our checking account, we kept increasing the balance as we added our investment, took out a loan and received some revenue. These were all debits to this asset account. When we bought office supplies, however, we used some of our cash, and thus, to decrease the account, we had to credit it. You will net the two sides of the account and end up putting the difference on the side in which it ends up – meaning, in the Checking T-account, you were at $500, then added $1000 in revenue to get to $1500. Then you netted this with the $200 credit to checking for the office supplies. Thus, you end up with $1300 left in the debit side. Logically, this makes sense – you took the money out of the account to get supplies so of course you're left with a smaller balance.

Once you get used to debits and credits, they really become second nature and help you to understand any business transaction. You'll get to the point where you'll know instinctively that when you book a transaction, you need BOTH sides of it – your debits and your credits – and they have to be equal. It's a very powerful concept that allows you to think your way through the most complex business transactions. When you just intuitively know that you can't make a journal entry unless your debits equal your credits, it will help you figure out how to think about any transaction you have in front of you.

3) Creating Your Financial Statements

Previously, in Chapter One, I created a simple BS and IS for you from the transactions outlined above. But now, if we were closing out the books for the period, we'd need to update our statements based on all the transactions.

Let's start with the Income Statement, which hasn't changed. There are only two I/S accounts in our ledger above that need to hit the I/S – Consulting Revenue and Office Supplies. Thus:

My Consulting Business
Income Statement
For the Period June 30, 20xx

INCOME		
Consulting Sales	$1000	
Total Income		$1000
EXPENSES		
Office Supplies	($200)	
Total Expenses		($200)
NET PROFIT		$800

Now, let's try to create the Balance Sheet, using the information contained in the T-accounts above.

My Consulting Business
Balance Sheet
As of June 30, 20xx

ASSETS		LIABILITIES	
Cash	$1300	Family Loan Payable	$400
Total Assets	$1300	Total Liabilities	$400
		EQUITY	
		Owner's Contribution	$100
		Total Equity	$100
		Total Liabilities & Equity	$500

This looks good, right? NO! This Balance Sheet does not balance!

Notice total assets are $1300 but liabilities and equity are only $500. We've violated the Basic Accounting Equation, since in this case A does not equal L + E.

What is missing? NET PROFIT!

Net Profit – on BOTH Financial Statements

Do you remember in Chapter One how I defined Equity as:

(1) What you'd have left if you sold off all your assets to pay off all your liabilities, or (2) the netting out of all the money you put into the company and all the money you've taken out and the profit or loss over time.

All we've done so far is look at definition (1). We need now to consider the second definition – profit or loss over time.

When we add Net Profit or Net Income to the Balance Sheet, it will all balance out.

<table>
<tr><td colspan="4" align="center">My Consulting Business
Balance Sheet
As of June 30, 20xx</td></tr>
<tr><td>ASSETS</td><td></td><td>LIABILITIES</td><td></td></tr>
<tr><td>Cash</td><td>$1300</td><td>Family Loan Payable</td><td>$400</td></tr>
<tr><td>Total Assets</td><td>$<u>1300</u></td><td><strong>Total Liabilities</strong></td><td>$<u>400</u></td></tr>
<tr><td></td><td></td><td>EQUITY</td><td></td></tr>
<tr><td></td><td></td><td>Owner's Contribution</td><td>$100</td></tr>
<tr><td></td><td></td><td>Net Income</td><td>$800</td></tr>
<tr><td></td><td></td><td>Total Equity</td><td>$<u>900</u></td></tr>
<tr><td></td><td></td><td>Total Liabilities & Equity</td><td>$<u>1300</u></td></tr>
</table>

This looks so much better. Now the Assets equal the Liabilities and Equity, and this balance sheet balances.

Notice that in this example, the Equity is:

1. What you'd have left if you paid off your liabilities – $1300 (cash) minus $400 (liabilities) = $900
2. The netting out of all the money you put into the company and all the money you've taken out and the profit or loss over time – $100 (what you put into the company) + $800 (the profit over time) = $900

This is the beauty of accounting and why it is truly amazing. Everything foots. Everything balances. If it doesn't, then you have some work cut out for you to right the universe again. But once you do you'll feel great! So few things in life just balance like this.

CHAPTER 3

Creating Your Own Chart of Accounts

This book is called *Easy Accounting*, because I really, truly believe accounting is easy. I hope I've demonstrated that so far. But accounting is also amazing because there are so many facets to it.

Types of Accounting

There is *financial accounting* which is accounting for external users. This is what we think of with public companies – they put out financial statements that have been audited or verified by Certified Public Accountants (CPAs) so that investors or creditors can see what's going on in the company and use that information to make decisions about investing.

Then there is *tax accounting* which is what my firm does. This is similar to financial accounting but with a specific set of rules set in the Internal Revenue Code.

Finally, there is *managerial accounting* which is what we've really been talking about so far. Managerial accounting is creating a set of financial statements and records that help the management of the company make decisions. Until you start tracking your books, how will you know that you're spending 90 per cent of your revenue on computer equipment? How will you know that all your revenue is in one line of business? You can use these insights into your numbers to make decisions about your business, such as what type of products and services to offer, what to spend your money on and how you should invest in your business.

Creating Your Accounts – Managerial Accounting

When it's time for you, as a small business owner, to create your own Chart of Accounts, be sure to keep in mind that you're doing managerial accounting. That is, you should set up the accounts that make sense in your business. Here are two maxims I have:

Put in as much detail as will be useful later on.
Don't hesitate to make categories that make sense to you.

Let's say you're running that hypothetical consulting business. Say you are selling your services at an hourly rate, and you're also selling 'packages' – a flat fee for a specific deliverable. It would make sense, then, to keep separate income accounts for both. Once you start tracking those, you might find you are earning only 20 per cent of your total revenue from hourly consulting versus 80 per cent of your revenue from these packages. It might help you decide, then, to phase out hourly consulting. Or maybe you will decide to increase your pricing on the packages. Either way, once you're armed with that information, you can start to make more meaningful decisions about the course of your business.

On the flip side, let's say you get really excited about tracking your expenses, and you decide the category 'Office Supplies' is not specific enough. You want instead to see what you spend on paper, pens and toner separately. You set up three accounts: Paper Expense, Pens Expense and Toner Expense. But when you get to the end of the year, you realize that it's just too much detail and isn't helpful, The total expenditures on those three categories in aggregate might only be 5 per cent of total costs, so in reality, who cares what you spend on pens? In that case, you have put in too much detail into your accounts. So, like I said earlier, put in as much detail as will be useful later on.

However, say for you a big cost is taking cabs from meeting to meeting. For some businesses, it might be fine to lump all travel into one broad Travel Expenses category. For you, however, you might use several: Taxi Expense, Mass Transit Expense, Overnight Travel Expense. This way, when you're looking at your Income Statement and your profit is not as high as you'd like it to be, you can really see where the expenses are adding up and begin to cut costs. Without the detailed information given to you in these specific accounts, you wouldn't have the information you'd need to make managerial decisions. Thus, don't hesitate to make categories that make sense to you.

The Exercises, Part One

Now that we've waded through the very basics of the accounting cycle, let's take a break and make sure this is all sticking. The way to do that is to have you practice making journal entries with debits and credits, posting them to their respective T-accounts, and then creating financial statements from them. Please do these problems and check your answers on page 41 when you're done. The problem sets get progressively harder as you go as we take away the helpful prompts or 'training wheels'.

Quick Quiz – The Basics

Complete the following chart showing how accounts are debited and credited. Use '+' to show increase and '-' to show decrease.

Balance Sheet Accounts | Income Statement Accounts

Assets   Liabilities   Equity   Revenue   Expen

Debit

Credit

Give the basic Accounting Equation below.

Now, get ready to do some journalizing!

Problem Set One – Includes Training Wheels

You are starting a babysitting business. You're going to make money by providing bab-ysitting services and will have some expenses as you get started. You'll also invest some money into the business and take on a small business loan for some working capital.

Create a journal entry for each transaction below. Assume all transactions happen on June 30, 20xx. Remember you need four things for a proper JE.

1. You start a babysitting business and invest $1000 in owner's equity, which is deposited into the company's checking.

June 30, 20xx

DR ____

  CR ____

To record owner's investment into the business.

2. You purchase some toys to have on hand for when you're babysitting. You pay $50 for the toys with your new company credit card.

June 30, 20xx

DR ____

  CR ____

To record expense of toys purchased on credit card.

3. You decide to take a bank loan to have more cash. You borrow $500 that goes into your bank account.

June 30, 20xx

DR ____

  CR ____

To record funds received from bank loan.

4. You purchase a website for the business. You pay $95 using your debit card linked to your checking account.

June 30, 20xx

DR ____

CR ____

To record expense of website.

5. You have your first client! You babysit for a full day and receive $150 in cash, which you deposit into your checking account.

June 30, 20xx

DR ____

CR ____

To record income earned and received.

Now, you'll take the next step in your accounting cycle – you'll transfer these entries from the general journal to your general ledger. Post your entries to these T-accounts.

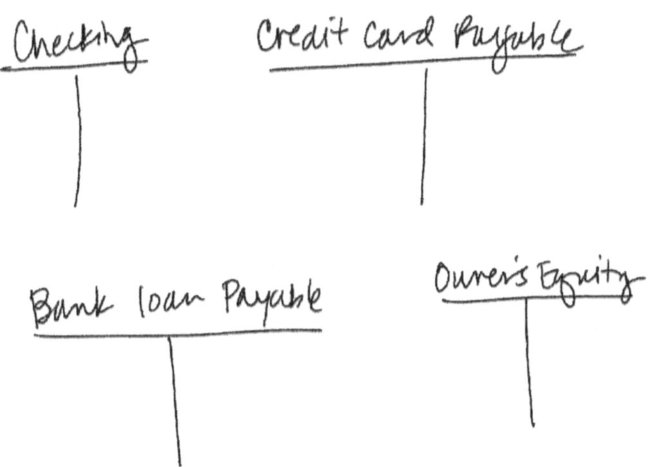

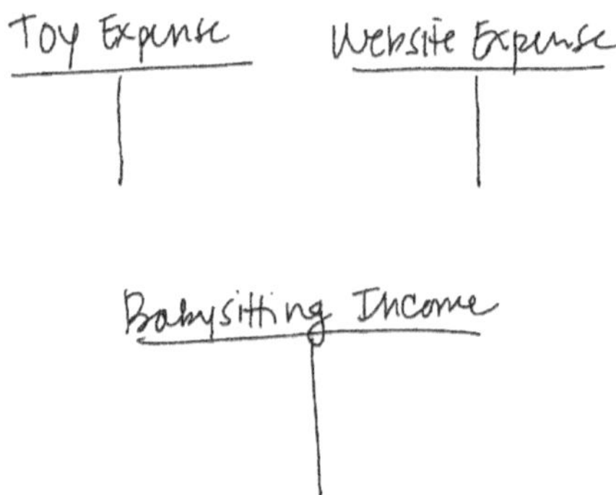

Finally, finish the I/S and B/S for these transactions. Remember each financial statement needs three things for its title.

<table>
<tr><td colspan="2" align="right">My Babysitting Business
Income Statement
For the Period June 30, 20xx</td></tr>
<tr><td>INCOME</td><td></td></tr>
<tr><td></td><td>________________________</td></tr>
<tr><td>Total Income</td><td>$______</td></tr>
<tr><td>EXPENSES</td><td></td></tr>
<tr><td></td><td>________________________</td></tr>
<tr><td></td><td>________________________</td></tr>
<tr><td>Total Expenses</td><td>($______)</td></tr>
<tr><td>NET PROFIT</td><td>$______</td></tr>
</table>

<table>
<tr><td colspan="2" align="center">My Babysitting Business
Balance Sheet
As of June 30, 20xx</td></tr>
<tr><td>ASSETS</td><td>LIABILITIES</td></tr>
<tr><td>________________</td><td>________________</td></tr>
<tr><td>Total Assets $____</td><td>________________</td></tr>
<tr><td></td><td>Total Liabilities $____</td></tr>
<tr><td></td><td>EQUITY</td></tr>
<tr><td></td><td>________________</td></tr>
<tr><td></td><td>Net Profit $____</td></tr>
<tr><td></td><td>Total Equity $____</td></tr>
<tr><td></td><td>Total Liabilities & Equity $____</td></tr>
</table>

Problem Set Two – Includes Training Wheels

Your babysitting business is in full swing, and a lot of your friends have seen how successful you are and decide they want to start a babysitting business too. To help them, you decide to open a side hustle as a business coach. You will make money by providing advice to folks who want to set up their own babysitting business, and you will invest some of your profits from the babysitting business into this new company.

Create a journal entry for each transaction below. Assume all transactions happen on June 30, 20xx. Remember you need four things for a proper JE.

1. You start your coaching business with your profits from day one of the baby-sitting business (which, if you did Problem Set One, you know were modest). You take the $5 in profits and invest it into capital stock, which is deposited into the company's checking.

June 30, 20xx

DR ____

  CR ____

To record owner's investment into the business.

2. You decide you're going to need more money to make this business happen. You don't want to take another bank loan on (because you still have one outstanding with your babysitting business), so you go to your mom and ask for a $250 loan. She gives it to you and you deposit that money into the bank.

June 30, 20xx

DR ____

CR ____

To record receipt of family loan.

3. You purchase paper, pens and staples for your new business from Staples. You spend $60 out of your checking account.

June 30, 20xx

DR ____

  CR ____

To record office expenses.

4. You make your first sale. Two of your friends purchase two hours of your time for advice in setting up the babysitting business. You determine that your hourly rate is $50, so you make and receive $200 and deposit it into the bank.

June 30, 20xx

DR ____

  CR ____

To record income earned and received.

5. You make a repayment to your mom with your first earnings. You give her $75 from your checking.

June 30, 20xx

DR ____

  CR ____

To record payment made on loan.

Now, you'll take the next step in your accounting cycle – you'll transfer these entries from the general journal to your general ledger. Post your entries to these T-accounts.

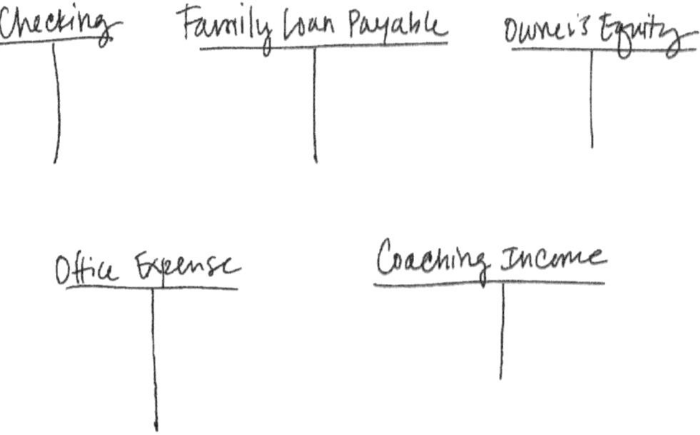

Finally, finish the I/S and B/S for these transactions. Remember each financial statement needs three things for its title.

My Coaching Business
Income Statement
For the Period June 30, 20xx

INCOME

____

Total Income $______

EXPENSES

____

Total Expenses   ($______)

NET PROFIT $______

My Coaching Business
Balance Sheet
As of June 30, 20xx

ASSETS   **LIABILITIES**

_______________   _______________________

Total Assets $______   Total Liabilities $______

                                     EQUITY

                                       ____

                                       Net Profit $______

                                       Total Equity $______

                                       Total Liabilities & Equity $______

Problem Set Three – No More Training Wheels

You are now the proud owner of a babysitting business and a coaching business, but your entrepreneurial spirit knows no bounds! You are really getting the hang of this accounting and bookkeeping, and you know that your new coaching clients need help with their books. So, with excitement in your heart, you decide to start a third business – a bookkeeping business!

Create a journal entry for each transaction below. Assume all transactions happen on June 30, 20xx. Remember you need four things for a proper JE. Note that in this problem set, the training wheels are off – no more prompts for your entries. You can do it!

1. You take some of the profits from your coaching business to fund this business – you open your new checking account with a personal capital contribution of $100.

2. You open an American Express card and charge the cost of a QuickBooks Online subscription. You pay $60 for the first three months' subscription with your new Amex.

3. You need to buy a laptop, and your brother has a laptop he doesn't use. He's willing to 'finance' it for you – he'll give you the laptop if you agree to pay him $400 for it, eventually. (Note, this is a loan!)

4. Your brother's friend runs a business and hires you to do bookkeeping for eight hours. Your rate is $75/hour and he pays you in cash, which you deposit into the bank.

5. You decide to take $100 from your checking to pay down the amount you owe your brother.

Now, use this page to post your entries to your T-accounts.

Use this page to create your Income Statement from your T-accounts.

Use this page to create your Balance Sheet from your T-accounts.

34

Problem Set Four – No More Training Wheels

Your friends and family are getting concerned with your workload as you are now running three businesses and you're busy. But your love for running businesses is paramount and you have another great idea for a company – this time a pet-care service to take care of adorable pets while their owners are away or to groom them as needed.

Create a journal entry for each transaction below. Assume all transactions happen on June 30, 20xx. Remember you need four things for a proper JE. Note that in this problem set, just like in the last one, the training wheels are off – no more prompts for your entries. You can do it!

1. You open a checking account with $50 of your own funds.

2. You purchase some leashes for the dogs, combs and brushes for grooming, and some treats to make the pets happy. You pay $35 for these pet supplies on your new company credit card.

3. You want to have a little more cash in the bank so you borrow $500 from your mother.

4.   You have your first client – you are paid $50 to take a cute pug for a walk. The client pays you in cash and you deposit it into the bank.

5.   You have your second client – you are paid $35 to visit, groom and play with a gorgeous Maine Coon. The client pays you with a check and you deposit it into the bank.

6.   You have your third client – you are paid $250 to groom a very grumpy and matted Persian cat named Bruiser. His frustrated owner gives you cash which you deposit into the bank.

7.   You pay $25 on your credit card bill from your checking account.

8. You repay your mom $65 from your checking account.

37

Now, use this page to post your entries to your T-accounts.

BECKY EGAN

Use this page to create your Income Statement from your T-accounts.

Use this page to create your Balance Sheet from your T-accounts.

The Exercises, Part One Answers

Quick Quiz – The Basics

Complete the following chart showing how accounts are debited and credited. Use '+' to show increase and '-' to show decrease in the white boxes and fill in the rest of the names of the types of accounts in the shaded boxes.

	Balance Sheet Accounts			Income Statement Accounts	
	Assets	Liabilities	Equity	Revenue	Expense
Debit	+	—	—	—	+
Credit	—	+	+	+	—

Give the Basic Accounting Equation below.

$$\text{Assets} = \text{Liabilities} + \text{Equity}$$

Problem Set One – Includes Training Wheels

You are starting a babysitting business. You're going to make money by providing babysitting services and will have some expenses as you get started. You'll also invest some money into the business and take on a small business loan for some working capital.

Create a journal entry for each transaction below. Assume all transactions happen on June 30, 20xx. Remember you need four things for a proper JE.

1. You start a babysitting business and invest $1000 in owner's equity, which is deposited into the company's checking.

June 30, 20xx

DR Checking 1000

CR Owner's Equity 1000

To record owner's investment into the business.

2. You purchase some toys to have on hand for when you're babysitting. You pay $50 for the toys with your new company credit card.

June 30, 20xx

DR Toy Expense 50

CR Credit Card 50

To record expense of toys purchased on credit card.

3. You decide to take a bank loan to have more cash. You borrow $500 that goes into your bank account.

June 30, 20xx

DR Checking 500

CR Bank Loan 500

To record funds received from bank loan.

4. You purchase a website for the business. You pay $95 using your debit card linked to your checking account.

June 30, 20xx

DR Website Expense 95

CR Checking 95

To record expense of website.

5. You have your first client! You babysit for a full day and receive $150 in cash, which you deposit into your checking account.

June 30, 20xx

DR Checking 150

CR Babysitting Income 150

To record income earned and received.

Now, you'll take the next step in your accounting cycle – you'll transfer these entries from the general journal to your general ledger. Post your entries to these T-accounts.

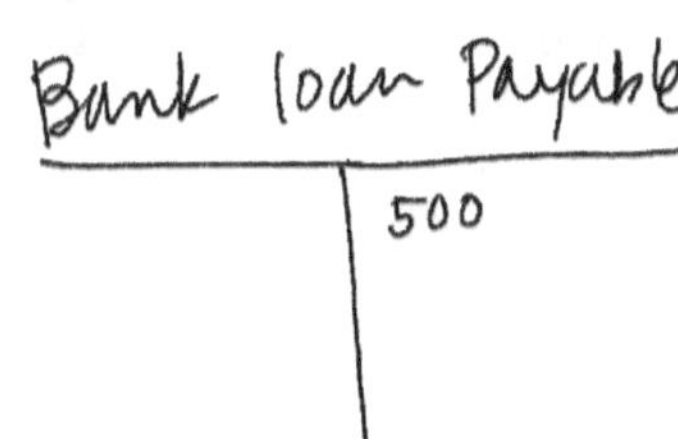

Finally, finish the I/S and B/S for these transactions. Remember each financial statement needs three things for its title.

My Babysitting Business
Income Statement
For the Period June 30, 20xx

INCOME

Babysitting Income 150

Total Income $ *150*

EXPENSES

Toy Expense   50
Website Expense   95

Total Expenses   ($ *145*)

NET PROFIT $ *5*

My Babysitting Business
Balance Sheet
As of June 30, 20xx

ASSETS

Checking

Total Assets $____

LIABILITIES

Credit Card Payable 50
Bank Loan   500

Total Liabilities $ *550*

EQUITY

Owner's Equity 1000

Net Profit $ *5*

Total Equity $ *1005*

Total Liabilities & Equity $ *1555*

Problem Set Two – Includes Training Wheels

Your babysitting business is in full swing, and a lot of your friends have seen how successful you are and decide they want to start a babysitting business too. To help them, you decide to open a side hustle as a business coach. You will make money by providing advice to folks who want to set up their own babysitting business, and you will invest some of your profits from the babysitting business into this new company.

Create a journal entry for each transaction below. Assume all transactions happen on June 30, 20xx. Remember you need four things for a proper JE.

1. You start your coaching business with your profits from day one of the babysitting business (which, if you did Problem Set One, you know were modest). You take the $5 in profits and invest it into capital stock, which is deposited into the company's checking.

June 30, 20xx

DR _______ Checking _______ 5 _______

CR _______ Owner's Equity _______ 5 _______

To record owner's investment into the business.

2. You decide you're going to need more money to make this business happen. You don't want to take another bank loan on (because you still have one outstanding with your babysitting business), so you go to your mom and ask for a $250 loan. She gives it to you and you deposit that money into the bank.

June 30, 20xx

DR _______ Checking 250 _______

CR _______ Family Loan Payable 250 _______

To record receipt of family loan.

3. You purchase paper, pens, and staples for your new business from Staples. You spend $60 out of your checking account.

June 30, 20xx

DR _______ Office Expenses 60 _______

CR _______ Checking 60 _______

To record office expenses.

4. You make your first sale. Two of your friends purchase two hours of your time for advice in setting up the babysitting business. You determine that your hourly rate is $50, so you make and receive $200 and deposit it into the bank.

June 30, 20xx

DR __Checking   200__

CR __Coaching Income   200__

To record income earned and received.

5. You make a repayment to your mom with your first earnings. You give her $75 from your checking.

June 30, 20xx

DR __Family Loan Payable   75__

CR __Checking   75__

To record payment made on loan.

Now, you'll take the next step in your accounting cycle – you'll transfer these entries from the general journal to your general ledger. Post your entries to these T-accounts.

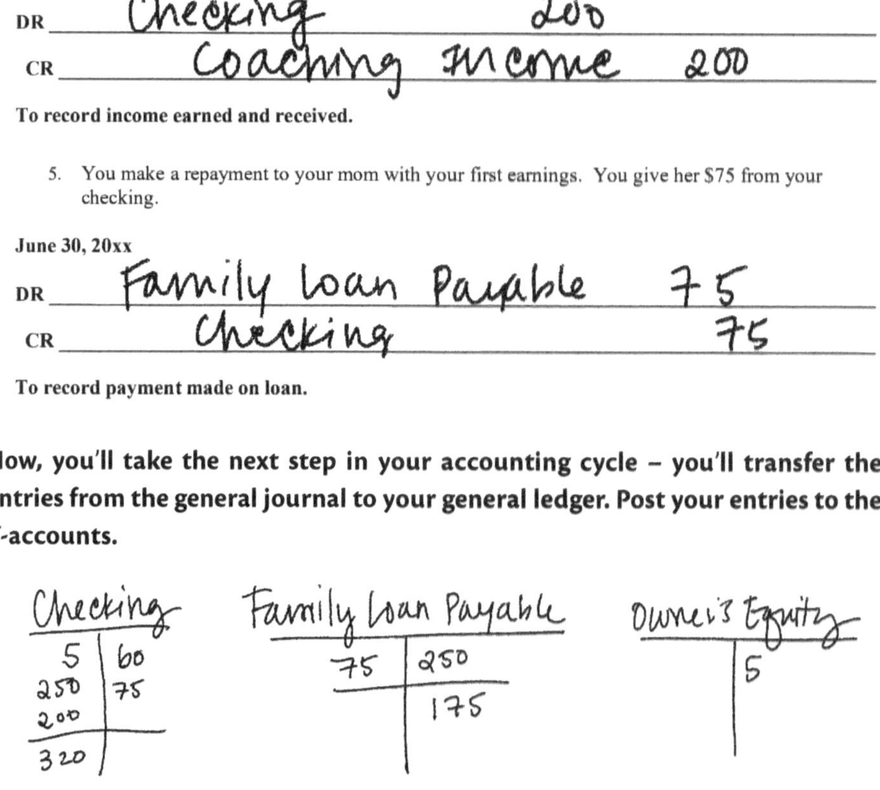

Finally, finish the I/S and B/S for these transactions. Remember each financial statement needs three things for its title.

My Coaching Business
Income Statement
For the Period June 30, 20xx

INCOME

Coaching Income   200

Total Income $ 200

EXPENSES

Office Expenses   60

Total Expenses   ($ 60)

NET PROFIT $ 140

My Coaching Business
Balance Sheet
As of June 30, 20xx

ASSETS

Checking   320

Total Assets $ 320

LIABILITIES

Family Loan Payable   175

Total Liabilities $ 175

EQUITY

owners Equity   5

Net Profit $ 140

Total Equity $ 145

Total Liabilities & Equity $ 320

Problem Set Three – No More Training Wheels

You are now the proud owner of a babysitting business and a coaching business – but your entrepreneurial spirit knows no bounds! You are really getting the hang of this accounting and bookkeeping, and you know that your new coaching clients need help with their books. So, with excitement in your heart, you decide to start a third business – a bookkeeping business!

Create a journal entry for each transaction below. Assume all transactions happen on June 30, 20xx. Remember you need four things for a proper JE. Note that in this problem set, the training wheels are off – no more prompts for your entries. You can do it!

1. You take some of the profits from your coaching business to fund this business. You open your new checking account with a personal capital contribution of $100.

> 6/30/xx
>
> DR Checking   100
> CR   Owner's Equity   100
> To record owner's investment
>   into business.

2. You open an American Express card and charge the cost of a QuickBooks Online subscription. You pay $60 for the first three months' subscription with your new Amex.

> 6/30/xx
>
> DR   Subscription Expense 60
> CR   AmEx Payable   60
> To record subscription expense.

3. You need to buy a laptop. Your brother has an old laptop he doesn't use and he's willing to 'finance' it for you – he'll give you the laptop if you agree to pay him $400 for it, eventually. (Note – this is a loan!)

> 6/30/xx
>
> DR   Computer Expense   400
>   CR   Family Loan Payable   400
> To record purchase of laptop.

4. Your brother's friend runs a business and hires you to do bookkeeping for eight hours. Your rate is $75/hr and he pays you in cash, which you deposit into the bank.

> 6/30/xx
>
> DR Checking   600
>   CR   Bookkeeping Income 600
> To record income paid in cash.

5. You decide to take $100 from your checking to pay down the amount you owe your brother.

> 6/30/xx
>
> DR Family Loan Payable 100
>   CR   Checking   100
> To record payment on loan.

Checking
| |
100 | 100
600 |
---
600 |

Owner's Equity
| 100

Am Ex Payable
| 60

Subscription Expense
60 |

Computer Expense
400 |

Bookkeeping Income
| 600

Family Loan Payable
100 | 400

300

My Bookkeeping Business
Income Statement
For the Period June 30, 20xx

INCOME
    Bookkeeping Income 600
        Total Income   600

EXPENSES
    Subscription Expense (60)
    Computer Expense (400)
        Total Expenses   (460)

NET PROFIT   140

My Bookkeeping Business
Balance Sheet
As of June 30, 20XX

ASSETS

Checking 600

Total Assets 600

LIABILITIES

AmEx Payable 60

Family Loan 300
Payable

Total Liabilities 360

EQUITY

Owner's Investment 100
Net Profit 140
Total Equity 240

Total Liabilities +
Equity 600

Problem Set Four – No More Training Wheels

Your friends and family are getting concerned with your workload. You are running three businesses now, and you're busy. But your love for running businesses is paramount and you have another great idea for a company – this time a pet-care service to take care of adorable pets while their owners are away or to groom them as needed.

Create a journal entry for each transaction below. Assume all transactions happen on June 30, 20xx. Remember you need four things for a proper JE. Note that in this problem set, just like in the last one, the training wheels are off – no more prompts for your entries. You can do it!

1. You open a checking account with $50 of your own funds.

6/30/xx

DR Checking 50
 CR Owner's Investment 50
TO record owner's investment.

2. You purchase some leashes for the dogs, combs and brushes for grooming and some treats to make the pets happy. You pay $35 for these pet supplies on your new company credit card.

6/30/xx

DR Pet Supplies 35
 CR Credit Card Payable 35
TO record purchase of supplies.

3. You want to have a little more cash in the bank so you borrow $500 from
    your mother.

    6/30/xx

    DR   Checking   500
        CR   Family Loan   500
    To record receipt of family loan.

4. You have your first client and you are paid $50 to take a cute pug for a walk.
    The client pays you in cash and you deposit it into the bank.

    6/30/xx

    DR Checking   50
        CR   Pet Income   50
    To record Income earned and received.

5. You have your second client who pays you $35 to visit, groom and play with
    a gorgeous Maine Coon. The client pays you with a check and you deposit it
    into the bank.

    6/30/xx

    DR Checking   35
        CR   Pet Income   35
    To record income earned and received.

6. You have your third client and you are paid $250 to groom a very grumpy and matted Persian cat named Bruiser. His frustrated owner gives you cash which you deposit into the bank.

6/30/xx

DR   Checking   250
    CR   Pet Income   250
To record income earned and received.

7. You pay $25 on your credit card bill from your checking account.

6/30/xx

DR Credit card payable   25
    CR   Checking   25
To record credit card payment.

8. You repay your mom $65 from your checking account.

6/30/xx

DR   Family Loan Payable 65
    CR   checking   65
To record loan payment.

Checking

50	25
500	65
50	
35	
250	
795	

Owner's Equity

	50

Credit Card Payable

25	35
	10

Family Loan Payable

65	500
	435

Supplies

35	

Pet Income

	50
	35
	250
	335

My Pet Care Business
Income Statement
For The Period June 30, 20XX

INCOME
    Pet Income   335
        Total Income   335

EXPENSES
    Supplies   (35)
        Total Expenses   (35)

NET PROFIT   300

My Pet Care Business
Balance Sheet
As of June 30, 20XX

ASSETS
Checking   795
Total Assets   795

LIABILITIES
Credit Card   10
  Payable
Family Loan   435
  Payable
Total Liabilities   445

EQUITY
Owner's Equity   50
Net Profit   300
Total Equity   350

Total Liabilities +
  Equity   795

Part Two

Easy Accounting Advanced

Welcome to Part Two: Easy Accounting Advanced. Remember a few times in the earlier chapters when I introduced a concept I said we'd get to it later? Welcome to later.

CHAPTER 4

Cash Versus Accrual

When we first talked about the income statement, we mentioned there were two methods of accounting – cash-basis accounting and accrual-basis accounting. The vast majority of small businesses use cash basis accounting, because it's simpler – and in small business, cash is king. However, let's take this time now to talk about the differences.

Accounts Receivable

Let's go back to our hypothetical consulting business. You work for one day and get a client to agree to pay you $1000. But let's assume that when you finish the day's work the client does not hand you a check. 'Send me an invoice, please,' the client tells you, which you do that evening. Two weeks later, you receive the check and deposit it in the bank.

So, you did the work today, June 30, but you get the check on July 14. Which date should you use to journal that transaction? Remember that when we create journal entries, we have to date them. In our example in Chapter Two, we booked the entry like this:

June 30, 20xx
DR Checking $1000
 CR Consulting Revenue $1000
To record revenue earned and received from Client A.

I don't know if you noticed it at the time, but the description I used to book that entry was, 'To record revenue EARNED AND RECEIVED from Client A.' In accounting (just as in life!), earning and receiving are two different events that do not have to happen on the same date.

What if you really wanted to book your revenue at the time the service was done? Maybe this would help you figure out how much you are really earning per week, month or year.

Let's make that entry. You'll date it June 30, and you know you are going to credit Consulting Revenue, right? But you also know that you need to have a corresponding and equal debit – remember, this is one of the basic tenets of accounting. You can't debit Checking, because you haven't been paid yet. So, what do you debit?

Enter Accounts Receivable! This is where you will keep track of all the money owed to you. It's also a very important feature in accrual-basis accounting. By using Accounts Receivable, you are able to accrue the income to your books, even if you haven't received it yet. Accounts Receivable (abbreviated as A/R) acts as a repository to hold all the revenue you've earned but have not collected yet. It's also a handy way to keep track of all the money you are owed so you can start calling clients who are late with payments.

June 30, 20xx
DR Accounts Receivable $1000
  CR Consulting Revenue $1000
To record revenue earned from Client A.

What type of account is Accounts Receivable? Well, we know it has a debit balance, because we used a debit to increase it. If you recall from Chapter Two, the only type of accounts that have Debit Balances are Assets and Expenses. It would not make sense to say A/R is an expense, so thus, A/R is an asset. This should feel right to you. We discussed in Chapter One that assets are expected to turn into cash in the future – and in the case of A/R, that is certainly true.

When you run your financials on an accrual basis, you would include in income anything earned in the period in question. So, in our example, the service was rendered on June 30 and paid on July 14. This means, that on an accrual basis, that income is properly included in the June income statement.

Can you see any possible downside to accrual accounting? Imagine that you are filing your taxes. You run your financials on an accrual basis, and you've just finished a large consulting project that is completed in late December 20xx. The client is expected to pay you in the following year. But you will need to include that income in your 20xx income statement and tax return – and by extension, you can now see that you will be paying tax on that revenue, even though you have not received it yet! For many small businesses, this can be an incredible hardship. This is why most small businesses use cash-basis accounting.

In cash-basis accounting, we 'count' income as income when it is received, regardless of when the service is rendered. In our prior example, the income is earned in June but received in July. Thus, it's income in July for cash-basis accounting. You might have done a service that took three years to be paid for. In cash-basis accounting, that income doesn't become income until the client pays you.

Accounts Payable

So we've discussed how income is counted in cash and accrual accounting. Let's look at the opposite side and talk about expenses. In today's world, many small businesses are able to put their day-to-day expenses on credit or debit cards or even to pay with ACH from their bank accounts, or they can even use old-fashioned cash. When this happens, the expense is booked immediately – DR Expense and CR cash, checking, or credit card payable.

But what if you incur an expense today that you don't have to pay for until 30 days from now (or 45 days, or 60 days)? Where does that expense belong? In cash-basis accounting, the expense is not counted until it's paid for. This is analogous to the way we treat income – it's not counted until it's received. In this way, as we said above, cash is king – we follow the actual money in or out to know when to book expenses or income.

In accrual-based accounting, this is not the case. When we discussed revenue, we stated that we needed to separate the act of earning income from the act of collecting income. In the same vein, with expenses, we can separate the act of incurring an expense from the act of actually paying for it.

Let's put this into action. Let's say you hired someone to create your website for you. The company created it exactly to your specifications and it looks great; you give the final approval to the company to make it go live, and then you receive in your email a bill from the company for this service. They are giving you 15 days to pay. How do you book this?

In cash-basis, we would debit Website Expense and credit how you paid for it – credit card, check, etc.

June 30, 20xx
DR Website Expense $300
 CR Credit Card $300
To record expense and payment of building website.

But in the accrual world, what do we do? Well, we know we'll need to DR Website Expense, but now we need a corresponding credit.

Have you figured it out yet? Yes, it's Accounts Payable! Just like with A/R, Accounts Payable (A/P) acts as a repository for all the expenses you've incurred but haven't paid yet.

June 30, 20xx
DR Website Expense $300
 CR Accounts Payable $300
To record expense of building website.

We know that A/P has a credit balance, and therefore we know it has to be a Liability, Income or Equity. In this case, it is obvious that A/P is a liability – it's something you owe to someone. As we said in Chapter One, liabilities are a drain on cash flow because you know you'll have to settle this in the future by paying it.

In this way, then, we've talked about the differences between cash and accrual accounting. If you are a small business, you'll most likely work on a cash basis – again, it makes the most sense!

The Matching Principle

Larger businesses, including all publicly traded companies, use the accrual method. The idea behind the accrual method is that it's meant to match revenues and expenses in each period and to give a better sense of the actual profitability of a firm.

Imagine you're running a small consulting firm. The firm is made up of you and one employee, and you pay both of your salaries on a bi-weekly basis (every two weeks). Imagine too that you have just one very large client that makes up all of your revenue. The client pays you sporadically for all the work done during the year. Now assume that you work all year on this client's work and you send out an invoice in December for $1 million to this client. (Nice going, by the way!) The client mails you a check and you receive it on January 15 of the following year.

On a cash basis, you'd have zero revenues in the current year! But you'd still have the full year of salary expenses for yourself and your employee, along with all your other costs (rent, supplies, travel, etc.). This would mean that your income statement for that period would show a very large net loss. Then, the following year, you'd pick up the $1 million of income. Further, assume you sent a bill to your client for the following year's work in January, and they pay another $1 million in February for the second year's work. Now, on a cash basis, you have $2M of revenue in this second year, when the work was done evenly throughout the two years.

It's very easy to see that this type of accounting will often distort the financial statements of a company. If you'd booked those revenues on an accrual basis, then you'd have $1M in revenues in the first year and $1M of revenues in the second year, and the costs for payroll and rent would go along with the revenue to show a picture of the profitability of the firm. This idea is called the matching principle – we want to match the revenues and expenses in a given period.

CHAPTER 5

Depreciation

Understanding the matching principle is useful for our discussion of this next topic, depreciation. Probably one of the simplest topics that is often the most confusing (!), depreciation is the matching principle exemplified. Let's take an example.

Let's say you want to buy a small condo to rent out for income. You know you're going to eventually end up with an income statement that shows rental income along with your operating costs. You assume it's going to look like this:

My Rental Business
Income Statement
For the Period January 1 through December 31, 20xx

INCOME

Rental Income	$24,000	
Total Income		$24,000

EXPENSES

Condo Common Charges	($6000)	
Property Taxes	($500)	
Supplies	($400)	
Repairs	($1600)	
Total Expenses		($8500)

NET PROFIT $15,500

Looks good, right? Right! But wait, you have to buy the condo, don't you? Oops. You have to spend $250,000 to buy the condo you intend to rent out. Where does this go on the IS? Do you deduct the whole cost in the year you buy it?

You can see right away that would be crazy! You'd deduct the whole $250k in year one and have a huge loss, but then you'd have higher profits in each of following years that you rented out the property.

But wait – real estate is an asset, right? That is what everyone calls it. So, if it's an asset, it belongs on the BS. So how do we get it on the IS?

This is where the matching principle comes into play. For assets that are long-term in nature – that have a 'useful life' of greater than one year – we need to employ a concept called depreciation.

In plain speak, depreciation is something you're likely think of in regard to a car – cars depreciate when you drive them off the new car lot. What does that mean? It means they go down in value. You'll see in a moment that depreciation in accounting means the same thing but with a slight variation – depreciation is when assets go down in BOOK VALUE.

Book Value

Wait, what is book value? Book value is how we record assets in accounting – the value they have on your books. In general, we record things at the price we paid for them. So, if you buy that condo for $250k but the next day the market tanks and it's worth only $100k, you leave the book value alone, as painful as it may be! The idea with accounting is that we keep things at book value to avoid having to keep adjusting them to differing market values. The same would go if property values skyrocket and your condo is now worth $500k – you'd still leave it on your books at the purchase price. In reality, even if the condo 'is worth' $100k or $500k, you still bought it for $250k, and it makes sense to use that as a marker of value on your books.

So, depreciation. We need to memorialize that the property is going down in book value, while at the same time we need to get some of the purchase price of the condo removed from your BS and onto your IS. Here is how we do that – depreciation expense!

Depreciation Expense

Depreciation expense is how we get some of the purchase price onto the I/S. As an expense, you know right away that it has a debit balance. So, when we debit depreciation expense, we are going to need to credit something to make the entry work. What do we credit?

The asset! In this case, we'd credit the condo. Remember that assets have a debit balance, so when we credit this asset, it's going to go down in value. Let's try an example.

December 31, 20xx
DR Depreciation Expense $9091
 CR Condo $9091
To record depreciation expense for the condo for year 20xx.

Where in the world did we come up with $9091? Stay with me, that part is coming! For now, assume this is the depreciation number.

When you move this J/E to your T-account for the condo, you're going to have a debit of $250k to get the asset on the books, and then you'll have a credit for $9091, which leaves you with a balance of $240,909. In this way, our book value went down for this asset, thus we depreciated it!

In practice, however, we do not generally credit the asset itself. Instead, we use what is called a contra account to hold this decrease in value. A contra account is any account that goes against another account and thus has an opposite type of balance (credit or debit) and is netted with the account it goes contra to.

With fixed assets, like our condo, we would typically create a new account called Accumulated Depreciation, and this would be a contra-asset account. Because assets have a debit balance, the contra-asset account would have a credit balance. However, credits still decrease the balance, so this Accumulated Depreciation account would always have a negative balance. Thus, when we net it against the condo asset to which it's contra, we decrease the overall value of the condo asset. But by creating a contra-asset account, we still keep the book value of the condo intact while memorializing what is left of the useful life of the asset.

On the balance sheet, it would look like this:

<table>
<tr><td colspan="3" align="center">My Rental Business
Balance Sheet
As of June 30, 20xx</td></tr>
<tr><td>ASSETS</td><td></td><td>LIABILITIES</td></tr>
<tr><td>Condo Asset</td><td>$250,000</td><td>xxxxx</td></tr>
<tr><td>Accumulated Depreciation</td><td>($9091)</td><td>EQUITY</td></tr>
<tr><td>Condo Asset (Net)</td><td>$240,909</td><td>xxxxx</td></tr>
<tr><td></td><td></td><td>Xxxx</td></tr>
</table>

An asset that also has a contra account associated with it is typically presented at net value, which is of course the difference between the purchase price and the accumulated depreciation – or the book value, the value at which it sits on your books.

Look again at the journal entry used to book depreciation:

December 31, 20xx
DR Depreciation Expense $9091
 CR Condo $9091
To record depreciation expense for the condo for year 20xx.

Notice also that this expense would hit your Income Statement so let's add it here.

<table>
<tr><td colspan="3" align="center">My Rental Business
Income Statement
For the Period January 1 through December 31, 20xx</td></tr>
<tr><td>INCOME</td><td></td><td></td></tr>
<tr><td>Rental Income</td><td>$24,000</td><td></td></tr>
<tr><td>Total Income</td><td></td><td>$24,000</td></tr>
<tr><td>EXPENSES</td><td></td><td></td></tr>
<tr><td>Condo Common Charges</td><td>($6000)</td><td></td></tr>
<tr><td>Property Taxes</td><td>($500)</td><td></td></tr>
<tr><td>Supplies</td><td>($400)</td><td></td></tr>
<tr><td>Repairs</td><td>($1600)</td><td></td></tr>
<tr><td>Depreciation Expense</td><td>($9091)</td><td></td></tr>
<tr><td>Total Expenses</td><td></td><td>($17,591)</td></tr>
<tr><td>NET PROFIT</td><td></td><td>$6409</td></tr>
</table>

Net income has gone down by the $9091 of depreciation expense, and this is a way to match the cost of the condo with the revenue it's earning for you.

Depreciation Methods and Useful Life of an Asset

Let's go back to the $9091 of depreciation expense. There are many ways to calculate depreciation expense. First, we need to talk about the useful life of an asset.

Because we're trying to match the cost of the asset with the revenues it generates (or has a tangential hand in generating), we first need to know how long it's going to be used and/or generating those revenues.

In tax accounting (what I spend my days doing), the Internal Revenue Service gives us classes of assets and assigns them useful lives, so you don't have to guess how long something is going to last – the IRS tells you what life to assign to it. Computers, for example, have a five-year life for tax purposes even though many people upgrade every two years, though I'm typing this on a seven-year-old laptop! Office furniture has a seven-year life, as do, interestingly enough, railroad tracks. Who knew?

Real estate that is used in producing rental income is first classified if it's being used as a residential property or a commercial property. Residential property in the US currently has a useful life of 27.5 years, while commercial property has a life of 39 years. This means, you will expense the full cost of the property of your condo over 27.5 years – it will take you that long to 'recover the cost' (you'll hear people talk about cost recovery which is often referring to depreciation) – of that investment.

Once you figure the useful life, then you get to figure which depreciation method to use. The simplest method is straight-line – you take the cost of the property and divide it by the number of years in its useful life, and that gives you your annual depreciation expense.

In our example above, we had a $250k condo that has a 27.5-year useful life, so the annual depreciation expense is $9090.91 – or the $9091 expense we used.

In straight-line depreciation, because we are dividing the purchase price by the number of years in its useful life, we get one number for the depreciation expense. This means that the depreciation expense will remain constant over the life of the asset. In some cases, this makes sense. For example, in real estate, it's probably right to assume that the depreciation should be the same each year. But in other things, let's say computers, we know that the usefulness of the computer is greatest right after you purchase it, and its value to you in generating income is likely to decrease over time. The IRS knows this too, and in tax accounting most non-real estate assets are depreciated using what is called MACRS (pronounced 'makers') – Modified Accelerated Cost Recovery System.

The mechanics of MACRS are outside the scope of this book, but suffice it to say that in this depreciation method – as with most other methods (double declining balance, sum of the years' digits) – you are taking a larger depreciation expense in the first year than in any other year, and the expense goes down slightly each year until the asset is fully depreciated. This would make sense in the example we used with the computer. When you buy a new computer, it's incredibly useful in that first year and likely has no problems that need fixing and is helping you generate a ton of output. But as the computer ages, in general, it's going to be less useful to you, and thus the expense is smaller each year.

There is another method of depreciation, which is called the Units of Production Method. In this method, which is most commonly used with manufacturing equipment, the gist is that a machine will produce a certain amount in its life. Thus, the number of units it produces in a given year is compared to the total number of units it's expected to produce over its existence. In years in which it's producing more units the depreciation expense is higher than in years in which it produces less. Thus, the depreciation expense is tied to the production of the machine, and we satisfy the matching principle.

Timing of Depreciation Entries

One final note on depreciation: how often do you need to book it? For most small businesses, you're going to book depreciation expense once a year, and that is likely during your meeting with your accountant. In this way, the tax accountant helps you determine the useful life of the asset and then tells you the number that you should debit in your books for the depreciation expense.

In practice, though, businesses might want to make entries to book the depreciation more often. This would be if the business were looking at interim financials on a weekly, monthly or quarterly basis. In this case, the business would make the entry at the end of the month for the month prior, so the monthly I/S properly showed a depreciation expense and more accurately reflected the profit of the company.

CHAPTER 6

Selling Stuff – Inventory and COGS

Another way in which we satisfy the matching principle is how we account for selling stuff. So far we've used service businesses in our examples. But what happens if, instead of selling your time, you sell stuff – water bottles, toys, cars, etc.? How do you account for the cost of the items you buy?

Inventory Asset

First, let's think about what it would be like to set up a toy shop. Sounds fun, doesn't it? You'd secure your space and then immediately start stocking the shelves. Imagine buying dolls, action figures, art supplies, games, books – you'd need to lay out a lot of funds to get the shop stocked and ready to open its doors. What do you do with the costs of those toy purchases?

Well, you spent money on them (out of your checking, say), so you know you're going to have to reduce your checking account balance and thus you'll credit checking. So, you know that to book the toy purchases to stock your shop, you'll need to debit something.

What would happen if you debited expense? Expense has a debit balance, right? Well, yes, but then you'd deduct the cost of all the toys you bought on the day you bought them – even if they stay in the shop for a week, a month or even years. That would not make sense! You'd have a huge loss in your first month of business and then your following years of income would not reflect the price you paid for the toys you are selling.

So, we know you can't expense them. You'll need to debit something else, so an asset is our only other choice. Remember in Chapter One we noted that assets are things that will turn into cash at some point? Well, your toys are really your inventory, and you will certainly turn these into cash at some point (hopefully with a nice markup!).

Thus, when you buy stock or items to keep in your inventory, you make the following entry:

June 30, 20xx
DR Inventory $10,000
 CR Checking $10,000
To record purchase of inventory.

When you transfer this entry to your T-account, the inventory account will have a debit balance that indicates you have inventory to sell, and if you ran a B/S at that moment, you'd see your inventory on your B/S, probably right after cash. Remember that assets are listed in order of liquidity.

Great, that makes sense. But what happens when you sell your first item? A little boy brings a toy truck to the register and he hands you cash. You'll certainly credit Sales Income, and then debit Cash on Hand. [Note that if his mom brought the truck to the register, she'd most likely have handed you the truck along with her credit card, and then you'd debit Credit Card Receivables not Cash on Hand. Credit Card Receivables is a holding account for the charges you run on your credit card processing system, more of which in the next chapter.]

June 30, 20xx
DR Cash on Hand $20
 CR Sales Income $20
To record sale of a truck.

So, you now have the income on your I/S. But you're down one truck in your inventory! And even though you sold that truck for $20, it cost you $7 to buy from your wholesaler, so just putting $20 on the I/S does not tell the whole story.

Cost of Goods Sold

Enter Cost of Goods Sold! Cost of Goods Sold is what is called a Mezzanine account, which I'll explain in a moment and which we referenced in Chapter One. Cost of Goods Sold is how we get the items out of Inventory and off the B/S and onto your I/S. The entry is simple and intuitive:

June 30, 20xx
DR Cost of Goods Sold $7
 CR Inventory $7
To record cost of goods sold for truck sale.

In order to fully tell the story of the sale of that truck, you actually need both entries. You can enter them separately, like we did above, or you can combine them like this:

June 30, 20xx
DR Cash on Hand $20
 CR Sales Income $20
DR Cost of Goods Sold $7
 CR Inventory $7
To record sale and cost of goods sold on June 30, 20xx.

Let's then take a look at what this looks like on our I/S:

	My Toy Store Business		
	Income Statement		
	For the Period June 30, 20xx		
INCOME			
	Sales Income	$20	
	Total Income		$20
COST OF GOODS SOLD			
	Cost of Goods Sold	($7)	
	Total COGS	($7)	
	Gross Profit		$13
EXPENSES			
	Total Expenses		$0
NET PROFIT			$13

Notice that here, we have added to our I/S the intermediary, the mezzanine account, of COGS. We call it a mezzanine account because just like the mezzanine in a theater, it's in the middle of income and expenses (or orchestra and balcony!). It allows us to see something new on the I/S: Gross Profit.

Gross Profit is an interim step to Net Profit. It represents the netting of the sales income and the cost of goods sold, so it represents the markup you have on the items you sell. In this case, we bought the toy truck for $7 and sold it for $20, so it stands to reason that we made $13 on it. In this hypothetical I/S, we haven't put in any other expenses, but once we did, we would net those with the gross profit number of $13 to get to net profit, which tells how profitable the toy shop actually is. Gross profit doesn't tell the whole story because we would need to add in other operating costs like rent, salaries for the staff, etc.

Recall too that the Inventory Asset T-account would be reduced by the item that is sold and is no longer in stock. Thus, if we had $10,000 of inventory before the sale, we would now have $9993 of inventory because we sold a toy truck that cost us $7 to buy.

In our example here, you've made the journal entry to book COGS after an individual sale. That is certainly the most accurate way to do it. But it's also incredibly time consuming. If you're using an automated accounting system like QuickBooks or a Point-of-Sale system, it's likely these entries are done automatically for you as part of the cash register function.

Another option is to do this entry once a year. In this case, every time you make a sale you'd simply book the sales income, but not book the COGS. And every time you replenished your stock, you'd debit your inventory asset, but you would not reduce it after each sale.

In order to get an accurate amount for COGS for the year (or month, or week, etc.), you'd use this formula:

Beginning Inventory
Plus Purchases made during the year
(Minus Ending Inventory)
= Cost of Goods Sold

This makes sense, right? You start with the $10,000 you bought in toys when you opened the shop, you add up any other purchases of stock you made, and then you figure what you have left at the end of the period – the result has to be the cost of what you sold throughout the year.

Note that this means you'll need a physical count of inventory at year end. This can be time-consuming, but might be less time-consuming than making the COGS entry after every single sale!

Other Uses for the Mezzanine Account

We've just gone through the most basic and standard use of the mezzanine account – retailers reselling items they've purchased for resale. But there are other uses for this very useful account too!

The first and most obvious extension of this account is for folks who manufacture their own items for sale. Assume you are making cat toys out of string, dowel and feathers. The simplest way to account for this would be to put all the costs of these items into an account called Inventory Asset as you purchase them. Then, you'd use the method above for determining your cost of goods sold by taking an ending inventory of what is left of the raw materials for your cat toys at the end of the period, and assuming that the difference represents your cost of goods sold. Does it also represent waste? Sure. Using something like string to produce a toy is going to produce some waste as you trim excess string. But in this case, it's likely the amount of string wasted is what is called immaterial.

The concept of materiality in accounting is about the amount of data that is useful in understanding your financials – at some point, something is so small, compared to the rest of the books, that it really doesn't have a bearing on the statements.

Imagine in our example of the cat toys that you waste $1 worth of string when making the toys. If you only have sales of $2, that $1 of waste is very material! But if you have sales of $1,000,000, then the $1 of waste is so small that by including it in COGS, you're not misrepresenting your financial statements. In fact, by including such a small amount, you're likely overburdening your financials with superfluous information.

There are other uses for mezzanine accounts. Remember that we are talking about managerial accounting – something you do for your own records and your own understanding of your business. In this case, you can use a mezzanine account for something other than Cost of Goods Sold. You can use a more general Cost of Sales account.

Cost of Sales is to differentiate certain types of costs from others. Recall that the Cost of Sales (COS) account would be a mezzanine account, and thus it is netted against sales to give you gross profit. You might like to see this number separated from your net profit – you might want to see a number for gross profit before you deduct rent, office supplies, etc.

Imagine you are a wedding photographer, and you book your sales as Wedding Photography income. But also imagine you have to pay another photographer to help you – someone commonly called a second shooter – who takes pictures from another angle, or at another part of the wedding, or while you're in the restroom. You might like to see the cost of paying this second shooter directly against your Wedding Photography income – after all, you would not have been able to collect that income unless you paid the second shooter. And this type of cost is very different in nature from the cost of maintaining your website or renting your office space. In this way, you can use this mezzanine account in ways that help you understand and run your own business.

CHAPTER 7

Other Assets, Other Liabilities

We've gone through the bulk of the basics of accounting so far – we've talked about income, expenses, and COGS; we've worked with checking accounts, credit card payable accounts and equity. We've hit all the basics you'll need to know to get going in accounting. But this next chapter will go through some other Asset and Liability type accounts that are commonly used. In doing so I hope to solidify your grasp of the basics of accounting (debits, credits, journal entries, T-accounts, and how they all fit together).

Other Asset Accounts – Receivables

Recall in the last chapter, we had a little boy who bought a truck at your toy shop. In that example, I told you the boy paid in cash but that if his mom were making the purchase, it's likely she would have used a credit card to pay for the toy.

If you've used a credit card (and if you haven't, who are you?), you may not have thought about the process of how a merchant accepts credit cards. Let me tell you, as someone who accepts credit cards in her business, once you process credit cards to receive payments, you'll never think about 'swiping and getting' the same way again! When a client or customer pays you with a credit card, the card transaction goes through instantly and that person's available credit for their card is reduced immediately by the amount of the charge. But the merchant does not receive this money right away. There is a several-day lag between when a customer swipes and when a merchant receives the money. Also, all of the swipes for a certain period of time (typically a day) are lumped together and deposited at once – but net of the fees. Yes, you knew who was really paying for your credit card rewards points, didn't you? The merchant! The typical fee for credit card processing is around 3 percent.

Let's walk through an example as to how this would work in our toy shop. You have three customers today, and each of them buys a few toys and pays with a credit card. You record each of these sales separately – note that. Let's also book the entries for the COGS at the same time.

You know you'll credit sales income for the sale of the items, but you're not getting cash or a check, so you don't debit cash or checking. Instead you will debit Credit Card Receivables. This is an asset account, which makes sense because we know it has to have a normal debit balance. We also know that this account is going to turn into cash at some point in the future – when Visa/Mastercard settle up with you and deposit the funds into your checking account, net of fees.

June 30, 20xx
DR Credit Card Receivable $15
  CR Sales Income $15
DR Cost of Goods Sold $5
  CR Inventory $5
To record sale and cost of goods sold for sale of doll on June 30, 20xx.

Then you have a second sale:

June 30, 20xx
DR Credit Card Receivable $45
  CR Sales Income $45
DR Cost of Goods Sold $12
  CR Inventory $12
To record sale and cost of goods sold for sale of stuffed animal on June 30, 20xx.

Finally, we have our third sale:

June 30, 20xx
DR Credit Card Receivable $10
 CR Sales Income $10
DR Cost of Goods Sold $8
 CR Inventory $8
To record sale and cost of goods sold for sale of book on June 30, 20xx.

Let's look at the T-account for Credit Card Receivables: first we'll debit $15 for the sale of the doll, then we debit $45 for the sale of the stuffed animal, and finally we debit $10 for the sale of the book. The total debit balance for Credit Card Receivables is $70 as of the end of the day.

Three days later, you'll get those funds deposited to your bank account. In nearly all cases, the amounts are lumped together for all sales in one period (typically a day) and net of fees. Assume in this case that the fees are 3 per cent – as we mentioned they often are – so the fees will be $2. Let's book the entry.

July 2, 20xx
DR Checking $68
DR Credit Card Processing Fee Expense
 CR Credit Card Receivables $70
To record deposit of credit card receivables into checking.

Note here that we are not getting the full amount charged – we're getting $68, not $70. So we know we need to debit the $68 to increase our checking by the amount of money we actually received. But to clear out the amount that was charged on credit cards and is sitting and waiting for us, we have to credit the Receivables account by $70. We can't make an entry that has debits not matching credits! So, we need to add the fees, which then makes sense of the fact that we didn't get all the money. That is where the $2 debit comes in – the credit card processing fee expense. This goes on the Income Statement.

For clarity, let's create an I/S for these few days of transactions. Assume that the shop was open for business on June 30, made those three sales, and then was closed and nothing else happened until the deposit of the credit card receivables on July 2.

My Toy Store Business

Income Statement

For the Period June 30 - July 2, 20xx

INCOME

    Sales Income $70

    Total Income $70

COST OF GOODS SOLD

    Cost of Goods Sold   ($25)

    Total COGS   ($25)

    Gross Profit $45

EXPENSES

    CC Processing Expense   ($2)

    Total Expenses   ($2)

NET PROFIT $43

Do you see how the credit card processing fee is an expense that affects net profit? This is because your customers have a choice of paying by cash or check as well, and thus it's not technically a part of COGS. However, some folks would prefer to put this into COGS to differentiate this from other operating expenses, and from a managerial accounting perspective, that is fine. Recall in Chapter Six, we talked about how the mezzanine accounts can be useful for you as a business owner to see how the business is doing? If lumping credit card processing fees into COGS so they are part of gross profit helps you understand your business, it's fine to do so.

Other Asset Accounts – Prepaids

Something like a Credit Card Receivable account is a great example of another type of asset account that you might encounter. Another example is something we call Prepaids.

In cash-basis accounting, for the most part, when we pay for something we expense it, regardless of when the service is rendered. In accrual basis accounting, however, this is not the case.

Consider for example your business insurance. Insurance usually runs annually and renews on your anniversary date of the purchase. So, while you probably look at your financials on a calendar year basis, your insurance might run from March to February.

On an accrual basis, we need to separate the insurance that is used in the current year to be expensed in the current year. In order to do that, the convention is to book all insurance payments to something called Prepaid Insurance and not to expense.

You get your bill for your business owners' policy on February 15, and it's due March 15 for coverage from March 1 to February 28 of the following year. To book this, on an accrual basis, we'll use Prepaid Insurance:

February 15, 20xx
DR Prepaid Insurance $600
 CR Checking $600
To record payment of insurance.

Do you see that this is a balance sheet transfer? We only moved money from one asset (checking) to another asset (prepaid insurance). In order to move the insurance to the income statement, we would need either a monthly or an annual accrual to take the cost of the insurance. If you pay $600 for an annual policy, in the absence of anything telling us otherwise, you'd be able to assume that the coverage cost $50 per month ($600 ÷ 12 months). Thus, you know that each month, you 'use' $50 of insurance and can expense it. That entry looks like this:

March 31, 20xx
DR Insurance Expense $50
 CR Prepaid Insurance $50
To expense insurance for March.

It's convention to book this at the end of the month because that is when the coverage is used, and by doing this, we then reduce the amount of prepaid insurance left, which makes sense, right? We paid for $600 of insurance and we used 1/12th of it in the first month the policy was in effect.

Other Asset Accounts – Longer-term Assets

We looked at two accounts that are going to change their balance fairly quickly – receivables and prepaids. Let's look at something that is going to have a longer life on your books – security deposits.

When you decided to open your toy shop, you first had to secure your retail location, and to do that, you probably had to put up a security deposit. Everyone who's ever rented an apartment or an office knows this drill – you typically need to give the landlord at least two months' rent as security so that you have some skin in the game of the place you're renting and thus are given an incentive to keep it in good shape.

Because this is something you are expecting to get back, you would not expense this amount when you put the deposit down. It instead lives on the balance sheet as an asset that you will keep there until you either use it or get it back.

June 30, 20xx
DR Security Deposit $2500
 CR Checking $2500
To record payment of security deposit.

We list assets on the balance sheet in the order of expected liquidity (turning into cash). Consequently, this is likely to be one of your last listed assets. Also note that listing this deposit on your balance sheet means it's not an expense. Similarly, when you receive the deposit back at the end of the lease term it's not income – it's simply the return of the deposit.

Other Liabilities – Trust Accounts

Up until now we've talked about three types of other asset accounts. Now, let's look at other liability accounts. One of the most common types of these are the 'trust' accounts, which hold the money you're collecting on behalf of various government agencies until it's time for you to turn them over.

The simplest of these to book is the Sales Tax Payable liability account. Chances are you live in a state that imposes a sales tax (at the time of writing only five states did not have a sales tax) or you've made a purchase that was subject to sales tax. The idea behind this is that the state government wants to collect revenue at the source of a purchase, and to do that, the vendor who is selling the item subject to the tax must collect the tax from the customer and hold onto it until remitting it to the government. Every state is different, but generally most states want the taxes turned over at a frequency that corresponds with how much you're collecting. In New York, for example, most filers start as quarterly (four times a year) filers, but depending on how much they collect, they may be asked to only file and remit annually, if they collect very little, or they may be asked to file and remit more often like monthly or weekly (if they collect a lot).

When you collect the sales tax, this is not income to you. It's also not your money – you owe it to the government. You hold onto it until you remit it, thus it's a liability and something that will be a drain on cash at some point in the future.

Let's go back to our toy shop. Imagine it's located in New York City, where the sales tax rate is 8.875 per cent. In our first sale of the day – the little boy who bought the truck – we need to add in sales tax to this transaction. Recall he paid $20 for the truck. Sales tax on this is roughly $2. Instead of handing us a $20 bill, he'll need to give us a $20 and two dollar bills. So we know we'll debit cash for $22, and we'll credit Sales Income for $20 – and the remaining $2 is going to Sales Tax Payable liability account:

June 30, 20xx
DR Cash on Hand $22
** CR Sales Income $20**
** CR Sales Tax Payable $2**
To record sale and payment of truck and sales tax.

Remember when we looked at the Credit Card Receivables account? The T-account kept getting larger with each sale made via credit card, and then eventually it was 'flushed out' by an entry to mark the deposit. Something similar happens with Sales Tax Payable. Each sale will add to this T-account (by crediting, of course), and then at some point we have to turn this money over to the government. Let's look at that entry, assuming the only taxable sale we had is that truck sale where we collected $2.

June 30, 20xx
DR Sales Tax Payable $2
** CR Checking $2**
To record payment of sales tax.

Other examples of this type of tax are payroll taxes. As you probably know, when you are on the payroll of a company, you don't get all the money you're supposed to be paid! Your employer is required by law to withhold 7.65 per cent of your check, right off the top, for your share of FICA (Federal Insurance Contribution Act), which is made up of payments to Social Security and Medicare. Your employer is also required to withhold federal and state income taxes on your check, depending on what settings you chose in your payroll documents (your W4, for example, that you likely filled out when you began work). This withheld tax is on top of the FICA payments. Similar to sales tax payable, payroll taxes are required to be remitted on a schedule that the government sets out with you. It is typically quarterly but often more frequent, depending on how much you remit at a time.

Let's look at an example here. Imagine you hire a sales assistant at your toy shop. You agree to pay him bi-weekly (every two weeks) $20/hour, and you'll pay him. He works 20 hours the first week and 17 hours the second week. Thus, you know you owe him $20 times 37 hours, or $740.

You are required to withhold 7.65 percent of this amount for his share of FICA (you'll pay that same amount too as your employer tax, but more on that later). His FICA is roughly $57. Assume too that you live in a state with no income tax (lucky you!) – but you will need to withhold federal income tax on his pay. The calculation of this is beyond the scope of this book (and honestly, it's beyond the scope of all businesses – please hire a payroll service to do this for you!!), but assume you need to withhold $70 for federal income tax for him.

From your perspective, as the employer, you are paying him the full $740. But you know you're not going to give him the full amount. So, book the full wage expense and show what you actually paid out, along with the amount that you'll owe in the future.

June 30, 20xx
DR Salary Expense $740
 CR Payroll Tax Payable $127
 CR Checking $613
To record salary expense.

Other Liabilities – Deposits

Let's look at one other type of account that comes up frequently in businesses – customer deposits.

Typically, when a client pays you money, it's for a service you've already rendered. But sometimes a client is going to give you a deposit for services to be rendered in the future – it's probably called a deposit if you're talking construction, or it's called a retainer in a law firm. This money hits your bank account, so we want to book it, but it's not yet earned on an accrual basis.

Imagine you are an attorney, and you charge $500 per hour for your legal services. In order to simplify your billing (and to make sure you get paid!), you require that clients give you a retainer of at least 10 hours of work before you begin with them. Thus, you are asking for $5000 up front when a new client starts working with you. In order to put this money on the books, but not yet count it as income, you'll use a Client Retainer liability account:

June 30, 20xx
DR Checking $5000
  CR Client Retainer $5000
To record retainer payment by Client X.

Then, once a week or once a month, you'll want to mark what proportion of the retainer has been earned so you can have that amount hit your income statement, and so you can see what is left on the retainer. In order to do that, you'll need to reduce the liability account, and to do that, we'll debit it. Say you worked two hours on the client's matter that week – you've earned $1000:

June 30, 20xx
DR Client Retainer $1000
  CR Legal Income $1000
To record revenue earned from retainer.

Thus, you'll reduce the balance in the retainer account from its initial $5000 to $4000 now. At some point, when this becomes too low, you might need to ask the client for a top-up on the retainer.

The Exercises, Part Two

You've now ploughed through the more advanced topics in accounting. Great job at making it this far! Just like in the Exercises, Part One, you're now going to have a chance to put your accounting skills to use by journalizing business transactions, then posting to T-accounts and then translating that to the financial statements. And, just like in Part One, you'll have some prompts in the first two Problem Sets here, and then we take the training wheels away for the last ones.

Problem Set Five – with training wheels

Remember that babysitting business from Problem Set One? It's thriving! You decide now to move to the accrual basis of accounting to better represent your income and expenses.

Create a journal entry for each transaction below. Assume all transactions happen on July 1, 20xx. Remember you need four things for a proper J/E.

1. You invest more funds into your checking account – $5000 from your own equity.

July 1, 20xx
DR ____
  CR ____
To record owner's investment into the business.

2. You work with a business attorney to help you create a client contract in order to protect yourself. The attorney sends you a bill for the work – $500 – and it's payable in 30 days.

July 1, 20xx
DR ____
  CR ____
To record legal expense payable.

3. You babysit for a new family. They pay you $150 on credit card.

July 1, 20xx
DR ____
  CR ____
To record income received and credit card receivable.

4. Suspend disbelief for a moment and assume that you receive payment for that credit card you swiped in item 3 in about three hours. The credit card processing fee is $5.

July 1, 20xx
DR ____
DR ____
  CR ____
To record receipt of credit card receivable and processing expense.

5. You purchase a new laptop for your business. You pay $2000 for it via your credit card. You decide to book it as a depreciable asset.

July 1, 20xx
DR ____
  CR ____
To record fixed asset purchase.

6. Suspend disbelief for another moment and assume that you will start depreciating the laptop today. It's got a useful life of five years, and you'll use straight-line depreciation.

July 1, 20xx
DR ____
  CR ____
To record depreciation of laptop.

7. You babysit for a new family that hopes to use your services a lot. You charge $600 for the day, and they ask you to send them an invoice. Normally you wouldn't do this but you decide to do as they ask because they have the potential to be a big client for you.

July 1, 20xx
DR ____
 CR ____
To record income.

8. Another family wants to use your services every day for an hour or two and doesn't want to have to worry about paying you every single time they have you come over. The father asks if he can give you a retainer of funds that he can draw down as you babysit for the family. You agree, and he gives you cash of $1000 that you put into the bank.

July 1, 20xx
DR ____
 CR ____
To record customer prepayment.

9. This same father from item 8 asks if you can stay and watch the kids for four hours. You agree, and you note that this will take $200 off his deposit with you.

July 1, 20xx
DR ____
 CR ____
To record income earned from customer deposit.

10. You make a $10 payment on your credit card.

July 1, 20xx
DR ____
 CR ____
To record customer prepayment.

Now, you'll take the next step in your accounting cycle – you'll transfer these entries from the general journal to your general ledger. Post your entries to these T-accounts.

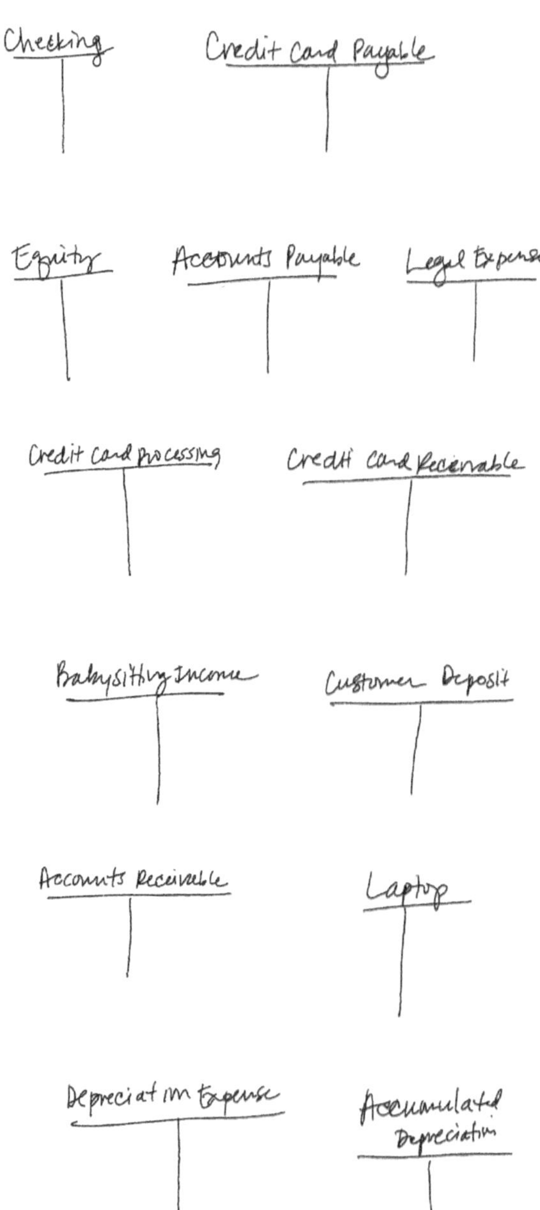

Finally, finish the I/S and B/S for these transactions. Remember each financial statement needs three things for its title.

<table>
<tr><td colspan="2" align="center">My Babysitting Business
Income Statement
For the Period July 1, 20xx</td></tr>
<tr><td>INCOME</td><td></td></tr>
<tr><td>_______________________</td><td></td></tr>
<tr><td>Total Income</td><td>$______</td></tr>
<tr><td>EXPENSES</td><td></td></tr>
<tr><td>_______________________</td><td></td></tr>
<tr><td>_______________________</td><td></td></tr>
<tr><td>_______________________</td><td></td></tr>
<tr><td>Total Expenses</td><td>($______)</td></tr>
<tr><td>NET PROFIT</td><td>$______</td></tr>
</table>

<table>
<tr><td colspan="2" align="center">My Babysitting Business
Balance Sheet
As of July 1, 20xx</td></tr>
<tr><td>ASSETS</td><td>LIABILITIES</td></tr>
<tr><td>_______________</td><td>_______________________</td></tr>
<tr><td>_______________</td><td>_______________________</td></tr>
<tr><td>_______________</td><td>_______________________</td></tr>
<tr><td>_______________</td><td>Total Liabilities $____</td></tr>
<tr><td>_______________, net</td><td></td></tr>
<tr><td>Total Assets $____</td><td>EQUITY</td></tr>
<tr><td></td><td>_______________________</td></tr>
<tr><td></td><td>Net Profit $____</td></tr>
<tr><td></td><td>Total Equity $____</td></tr>
<tr><td></td><td>Total Liabilities & Equity $____</td></tr>
</table>

Problem Set Six – Includes Training Wheels

Remember how in Chapter Six, we said it'd be fun to set up a toy shop? Well, good news – you've decided to set up a toy shop!

Create a journal entry for each transaction below. Assume all transactions happen on July 1, 20xx. Remember you need four things for a proper J/E.

1. You open your checking account with a deposit of $10,000 – $5000 from your own equity and $5000 from a Small Business Association loan.

July 1, 20xx

DR ____

  CR ____

  CR ____

To record owner's investment into the business and loan proceeds.

2. You need to stock your shop with toys, and you place a large order for inventory from a toy wholesaler. You purchase $3000 worth of toys and the bill is due in 30 days.

July 1, 20xx

DR ____

  CR ____

To record purchase of inventory.

3. You need to secure a retail location. The landlord asks for $4500 up front – $1500 is this month's rent and $3000 is a security deposit. You write him a check.

July 1, 20xx

DR ____

DR ____

  CR ____

To record payment of one month's rent and security deposit.

4. You make your first sale. A little girl buys a truck for $20. The sales tax on this item is $1. She gives you the full amount in cash and you put it in the register. You also decide you will book your COGS entry with each sale. The truck cost you $5.

July 1, 20xx
DR ____
  CR ____
  CR ____
DR ____
  CR ____
To record cash sale, sales tax and COGS/inventory.

5. You make another sale. A dad comes in to buy a lot of gifts for all the upcoming birthday parties his kids will attend. He spends $500 on the toys, and the sales tax you collect is $25. The toys cost you $125 and you book COGS now.

July 1, 20xx
DR ____
  CR ____
  CR ____
DR ____
  CR ____
To record credit card sale, sales tax and COGS/inventory.

6. You hire an employee to help you with the shop. Assume you will pay him in cash, daily (suspend disbelief here!). His wage is $15/hr, and he works six hours today. The payroll taxes on this will be $19.

July 1, 20xx
DR ____
  CR ____
  CR ____
To record salary expense.

7. You receive a bill for your workers' compensation insurance – it's $500 and you pay for it with your credit card. You will book separately the use of the insurance.

July 1, 20xx
DR ____
 CR ____
To record payment of workers' compensation insurance.

8. Because your new employee worked today and you paid him, you decide to book the insurance expense for today. Assume, for this exercise, that the insurance 'used' today is $3.

July 1, 20xx
DR ____
 CR ____
To record workers' compensation insurance expense for the day.

9. You make a payment to your state sales tax agency for $10 out of your checking account.

July 1, 20xx
DR ____
 CR ____
To record payment of sales tax payable.

10. You make one last sale before closing for the day. A girl buys a truck for $40, sales tax is $2, and she gives you cash. The truck cost you $10.

July 1, 20xx
DR ____
 CR ____
 CR ____
DR ____
 CR ____
To record cash sale, sales tax and COGS/inventory.

Now, you'll take the next step in your accounting cycle – you'll transfer these entries from the general journal to your general ledger. Post your entries to these T-accounts.

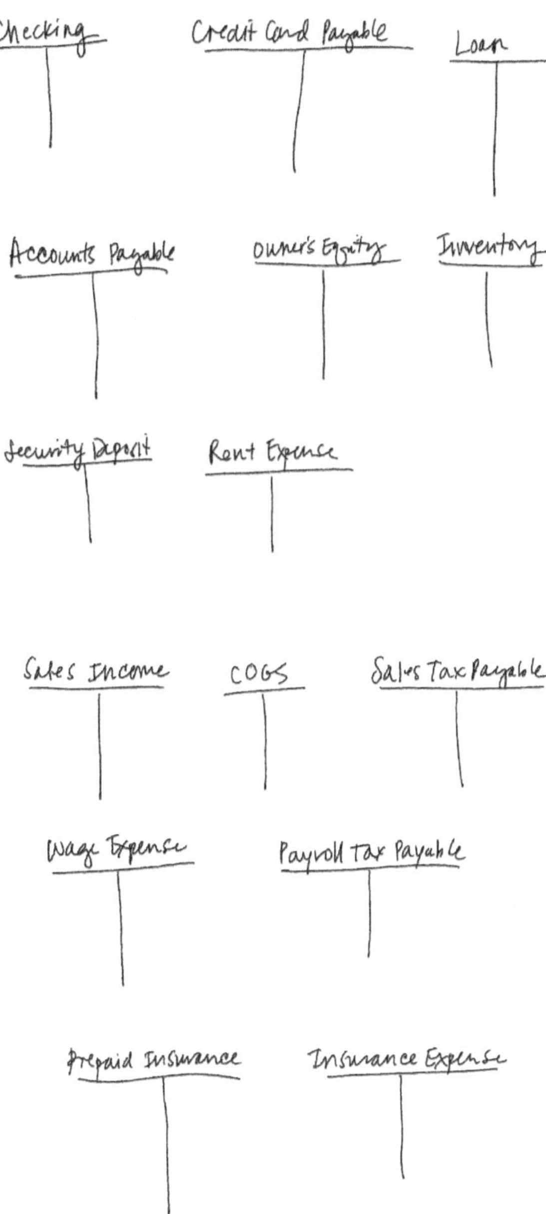

Finally, finish the I/S and B/S for these transactions. Remember each financial statement needs three things for its title.

My Toy Store Business
Income Statement
For the Period July 1, 20xx

INCOME

____

Total Income $______

COST OF GOODS SOLD

____

Total COGS   ($______)

GROSS PROFIT $______

EXPENSES

____

____

____

Total Expenses   ($______)

NET PROFIT $______

My Toy Store Business
Balance Sheet
As of July 1, 20xx

ASSETS	LIABILITIES
__________	__________
__________	__________
__________	__________
__________	__________
	__________
Total Assets $____	Total Liabilities $____
	EQUITY
	__________
	Net Profit $____
	Total Equity $____
	Total Liabilities & Equity $____

Problem Set Seven – No More Training Wheels

This time we're back to our bookkeeping business in Problem Set Three. You're killing it here, and you decide to move to accrual basis.

Create a journal entry for each transaction below. Assume all transactions happen on July 1, 20xx. Remember you need four things for a proper J/E.

1. You work with a business attorney to help you create a client contract. The attorney sends you a $300 bill for the work and it's payable in 15 days.

2. You take on a new client. His books are a mess and he needs you to clean them up. You decide to create a new income account for this so you can track this income separately from your monthly bookkeeping income. You will charge the client $1000 for the work and send him an invoice, payable in 15 days.

3. Your longest-running client wants to put some funds on account with you as a retainer so she can call you when she needs to. She pays you $3000 as a retainer and she puts it on her credit card.

4. Suspend disbelief for a moment and assume that you receive payment for that credit card you swiped in item 3 in about three hours. The credit card processing fee is $90.

5. You take on a new office space for your business. The landlord asks for $1250 as a security deposit. You pay for it with your credit card.

6. You need a new laptop for your business. You buy one for $1500 using your checking account.

7. Suspend disbelief for another moment and assume that you will start depreciating the laptop today. It's got a useful life of five years, and you'll use straight-line depreciation.

8. Your client who gave you the retainer calls you for an hour's work. You charge $100 and take it from the retainer.

9. You decide to take out a business owner's insurance policy, which will cover you from July 1 through June 30 of the following year. The $500 bill for the policy arrives via email and it's payable in 30 days.

10. Your client pays you $300 for three hours of bookkeeping. She pays via check and you deposit it.

Now, use this page to post your entries to your T-accounts.

BECKY EGAN

Use this page to create your Income Statement from your T-accounts.

99

Use this page to create your Balance Sheet from your T-accounts.

Problem Set Eight – No More Training Wheels

To bring it all home, we will revisit your pet care business from Problem Set Four.

Create a journal entry for each transaction below. Assume all transactions happen on July 1, 20xx. Remember you need four things for a proper J/E.

1. You decide that in addition to selling your time for pet care services, you'll also sell pet products to your clients. As such, you know you need to bulk up your inventory, and in preparation for this you obtain a loan from your bank in the amount of $3000.

2. Now it's time to buy that inventory. You place an order for $2500 worth of cat toys, dog toys, leashes, brushes – the works. You put this on your business credit card.

3. Your new client has five dogs and wants a lot of dog-walking while she's at work. To get started she agrees to give you a retainer for about one week's walking, or $250. She pays via check, which you deposit into the bank.

4. You are out on a dog walk later that day, and a leash breaks! Quickly, you use a spare that you had in your bag. You had intended to sell this leash, so it was sitting in Inventory, but at this point you need to expense it as a Pet Care Expense for $5.

5. You get a call from a cat owner who needs some cat grooming. While at the appointment, you not only charge the client for the grooming service ($45), but you also sell him a new de-matting brush for $10 and collect $1 in sales tax. The brush cost you $3. The client pays cash.

6. The client in item 3 calls you for an unscheduled dog walk, for which you take $30 out of her retainer.

7. Unfortunately, your commercial doggie dryer breaks! You call the pet supply store and order a new one for $400. They give it to you on store credit.

8. Suspend disbelief and assume you need to depreciate this doggie dryer. It has a useful life of 10 years and you'll use straight-line depreciation.

9. You make a payment of $25 to your business credit card.

10. While out on a dog walk, a prospect asks you about the collars on the dogs. Later that day, the prospect calls you to buy 10 collars for her dogs. Each collar retails for $28, and you collect that money in addition to $10 in sales tax. Each collar cost you $12, and you book COGS immediately.

Now, use this page to post your entries to your T-accounts.

104

Use this page to create your Income Statement from your T-accounts.

Use this page to create your Balance Sheet from your T-accounts.

The Exercises, Part Two – ANSWERS

Problem Set Five – Includes Training Wheels

Remember that babysitting business from Problem Set One? It's thriving! You decide now to move to accrual-basis accounting to better represent your income and expenses.

Assume you are beginning year two, and in your T-accounts you have $100 in the bank and $100 in Retained Earnings. This will be all that is on your balance sheet when you open the year on July 1, 20xx.

Create a journal entry for each transaction below. Assume all transactions happen on July 1, 20xx. Remember you need four things for a proper J/E.

1. You invest more funds into your checking account - $5000 from your own equity.

July 1, 20xx

DR _Checking_ 5000
CR _Equity_ 5000

To record owner's investment into the business.

2. You work with a business attorney to help you create a client contract in order to protect yourself. The attorney sends you a bill for the work - $500 - and it's payable in 30 days.

July 1, 20xx

DR _Legal Expense_ 500
CR _Accounts Payable_ 500

3. To record legal expense payable.

3. You babysit for a new family. They pay you $150 on credit card.

July 1, 20xx

DR _Credit Card Receivable_ 150
CR _Babysitting Income_ 150

To record income received and credit card receivable.

4. Suspend disbelief for a moment and assume that you receive payment for that credit card you swiped in item 3 in about three hours. The credit card processing fee is $5.

July 1, 20xx

DR _Checking_ 145
DR _CC processing Fee_ 5
CR _Credit card Receivable_ 150

To record receipt of credit card receivable and processing expense.

5. You purchase a new laptop for your business. You pay $2000 for it via your credit card. You decide to book it as a depreciable asset.

July 1, 20xx

DR   Laptop   2000

CR   Credit card payable   2000

To record fixed asset purchase.

6. Suspend disbelief for another moment and assume that you will start depreciating the laptop today. It's got a useful life of five years, and you'll use straight line depreciation.

July 1, 20xx

DR   Depreciation Expense   400

CR   Accumulated Depreciation   400

To record depreciation of laptop.

7. You babysit for a new family that hopes to use your services a lot. You charge $600 for the day, and they ask that you send them an invoice. Normally you wouldn't do this but you decide to do as they ask because they have the potential to be a big client for you.

July 1, 20xx

DR   Accounts Receivable   600

CR   Babysitting Income   600

To record income.

8. Another family wants to use your services every day for an hour or two and doesn't want to have to worry about paying you every single time they have you come over. The father asks if he can give you a retainer of funds that he can draw down on as you babysit for the family. You agree, and he gives you cash of $1000 that you put into the bank.

July 1, 20xx

DR   Checking   1000

CR   Client Deposit   1000

To record customer prepayment.

9. This same father from item 8 asks if you can stay and watch the kids for two hours. You agree, and you note that this will take $100 off his deposit with you.

July 1, 20xx

DR   Client Deposit   100

CR   Babysitting Income   100

To record income earned from customer deposit.

10. You make a $10 payment on your credit card.

July 1, 20xx

DR   Credit card payable   10

CR   Checking   10

To record customer prepayment.

Now, you'll take the next step in your accounting cycle – you'll transfer these entries from the general journal to your general ledger. Post your entries to these T-accounts.

Checking			Credit Card Payable	
5000	10		10	2000
145				1990
1000				
6135				

Equity		Accounts Payable		Legal Expense	
	5000		500	500	

Credit Card Processing		Credit Card Receivable	
5		150	150
		0	

Babysitting Income		Customer Deposit	
	150	200	1000
	600		800
	200		
	950		

Accounts Receivable		Laptop	
600		2000	

Depreciation Expense		Accumulated Depreciation	
400			400

Finally, finish the I/S and B/S for these transactions. Remember each financial statement needs three things for its title.

My Babysitting Business
Income Statement
For the Period July 1, 20xx

INCOME

Babysitting Income

Total Income $ _950_

EXPENSES

Legal Expense (500)

Credit Card Processing (5)

Depreciation (400)

Total Expenses ($_90_5)

NET PROFIT $ _45_

My Babysitting Business
Balance Sheet
As of July 1, 20xx

ASSETS

Checking 6135

CC Receivable 0

Accounts Rec. 600

Laptop 2000
A/Dep. (400), net 1600

Total Assets $_8335_

LIABILITIES

Accounts Payable 500

CC Payable 1990

Client Deposit 800

Total Liabilities $_3290_

EQUITY

Owner's Equity 5000

Net Profit $_45_

Total Equity $_5045_

Total Liabilities & Equity $_8535_

Problem Set Six – Includes Training Wheels

Remember how in Chapter Six, we said it'd be fun to set up a toy shop? Well, good news – you decided to set up a toy shop!

Create a journal entry for each transaction below. Assume all transactions happen on July 1, 20xx. Remember you need four things for a proper J/E.

1. You open your checking account with a deposit of $10,000 - $5000 from your own equity and $5000 from a Small Business Association loan.

July 1, 20xx

DR	Checking	10,000
CR	Equity	5000
CR	Loan Payable	5000

To record owner's investment into the business and loan proceeds.

2. You need to stock your shop with toys, and you place a large order for inventory from a toy wholesaler. You purchase $3000 worth of toys and the bill is due in 30 days.

July 1, 20xx

DR	Inventory	3000
CR	Accounts Payable	3000

To record purchase of inventory.

3. You need to obtain a retail location. The landlord asks for $4500 up front - $1500 is this month's rent, and $3000 is a security deposit. You write him a check.

July 1, 20xx

DR	Rent Expense	1500
DR	Security Deposit	3000
CR	Checking	4500

To record payment of one month's rent and security deposit.

4. You make your first sale. A little girl buys a truck for $20. The sales tax on this item is $1. She gives you the full amount in cash and you put it in the register. You also decide you will book your COGS entry with each sale. The truck cost you $5.

July 1, 20xx

DR	Checking	21
CR	Sales Income	20
CR	Sales Tax Payable	1
DR	COGS	5
CR	Inventory	5

To record cash sale, sales tax, and COGS/inventory.

5. You make another sale. A dad comes in to buy a lot of gifts for all the upcoming birthday parties his kids will attend. He spends $500 on the toys, and the sales tax you collect is $25. The toys cost you $125 and you book COGS now.

July 1, 20xx

DR	Checking	525
CR	Sales Income	500
CR	Sales Tax Payable	25
DR	COGS	125
CR	Inventory	125

To record credit card sale, sales tax, and COGS/inventory.

6. You hire an employee to help you with the shop. Assume that you will pay him in cash, daily (suspend disbelief here!). His wage is $15/hr, and he works 6 hours today. The payroll taxes on this will be $19.

July 1, 20xx

DR	Wage Expense	90
CR	Payroll Tax Payable	19
CR	Checking	71

To record salary expense.

7. You receive a bill for your workers' compensation insurance - it's $500 and you pay it on your credit card. You will book separately the use of the insurance.

July 1, 20xx

DR	Prepaid Insurance	500
CR	Credit Card Payable	500

To record payment of workers' compensation insurance.

8. Because your new employee worked today and you paid him, you decide to book the insurance expense for today. Assume, for this exercise, that the insurance "used" today is $3.

July 1, 20xx

DR	Insurance Expense	3
CR	Prepaid Insurance	3

To record workers' compensation insurance expense for the day.

9. You make a payment to your state sales tax agency for $10 out of your checking account.

July 1, 20xx

DR	Sales Tax Payable	10
CR	Checking	10

To record payment of sales tax payable.

10. You make one last sale before closing for the day. A girl buys a truck for $40, sales tax is $2, and she gives you cash. The truck cost you $10.

July 1, 20xx

DR Checking 42
CR Sales Income 40
CR Sales Tax Payable 2
DR COGS 10
CR Inventory 10

To record cash sale, sales tax, and COGS/inventory.

Now, you'll take the next step in your accounting cycle – you'll transfer these entries from the general journal to your general ledger. Post your entries to these T-accounts.

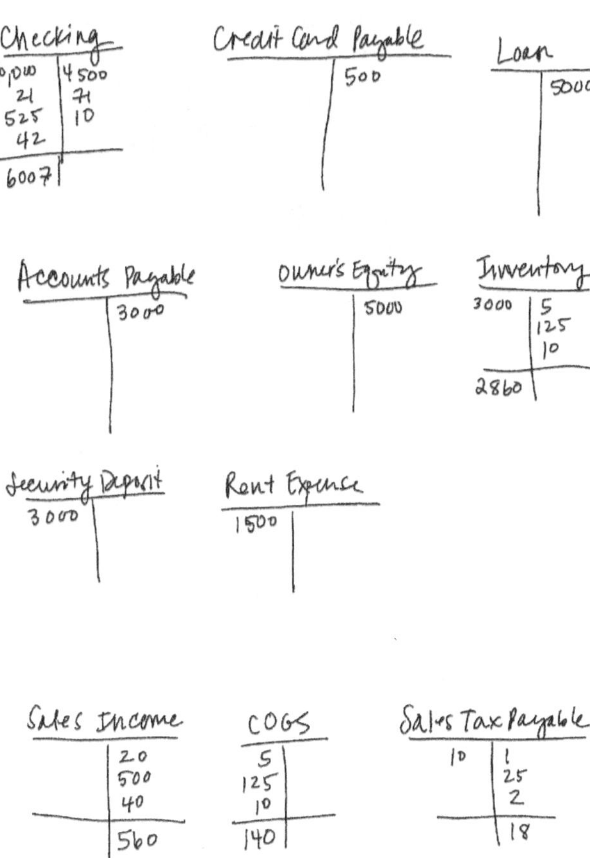

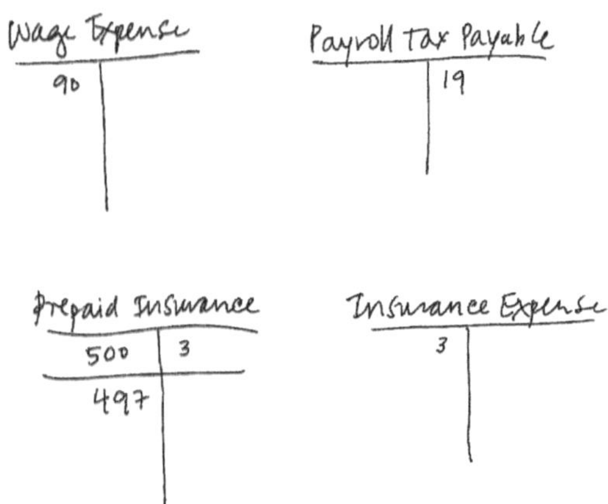

Finally, finish the I/S and B/S for these transactions. Remember each financial statement needs three things for its title.

My Toy Store Business
Income Statement
For the Period July 1, 20xx

INCOME

Sales Income

Total Income $ 560

COST OF GOODS SOLD

COGS

Total COGS   ($ 140)

GROSS PROFIT $ 420

EXPENSES

Wage Expense   (90)

Rent Expense   (1500)

Insurance Expense   (3)

Total Expenses   ($ 1593)

NET PROFIT $ (1173)

My Toy Store Business
Balance Sheet
As of July 1, 20xx

ASSETS

Checking 6007
Inventory 2860
Prepaid Ins. 497
Security Dep 3000

Total Assets $ 12,364

LIABILITIES

Accounts Payable 3000
Credit Card Payable 500
Sales tax payable 18
Payroll Tax payable 19
Loan 5000

Total Liabilities $ 8537

EQUITY

Owners Equity 5000
Net Profit $ (1173)

Total Equity $ 3827

Total Liabilities & Equity $ 12,364

Problem Set Seven – No More Training Wheels

This time we're back to our bookkeeping business in Problem Set Three. You're killing it here, and you decide to move to accrual basis.

Create a journal entry for each transaction below. Assume all transactions happen on July 1, 20xx. Remember you need four things for a proper J/E.

1. You work with a business attorney to help you create a client contract. The attorney sends you a $300 bill for the work, and it's payable in 15 days.

> 7/1/xx
>
> DR Legal Expense 300
>   CR Accounts Payable 300
> To book legal expense.

2. You take on a new client. His books are a mess and he needs you to clean them up. You decide to create a new income account for this so you can track this income separately from your monthly bookkeeping income. You will charge the client $1000 for the work and send him an invoice, payable in 15 days.

> 7/1/xx
>
> DR Accounts Receivable 1000
>   CR Clean Up Income 1000
> To book income earned.

3. Your longest-running client wants to put some funds on account with you as a retainer so she can call you when she needs to. She pays you $3000 as a retainer and she puts it on her credit card.

> 7/1/xx
>
> DR Credit Card Receivable 3000
>   CR Client Deposit 3000
> to book deposit received.

4. Suspend disbelief for a moment and assume that you receive payment for that credit card you swiped in item 3 in about three hours. The credit card processing fee is $90.

7/11xx

DR Checking   2910
DR Credit Card Fee   90
    CR Credit Card Receivable 3000
To book receipt of CC receivable.

5. You take on a new office space for your business. The landlord asks for $1250 as a security deposit. You pay for it with your credit card.

7/11xx

DR Security Deposit   1250
    CR Credit Card Payable 1250
To book security deposit.

6. You need a new laptop for your business. You buy one for $1500 using your checking account.

7/11xx

DR Laptop   1500
    CR Checking   1500
To book purchase of laptop.

7. Suspend disbelief for another moment and assume that you will start depreciating the laptop today. It's got a useful life of five years, and you'll use straight-line depreciation.

7/1/xx

DR Depreciation Expense   300
    CR Accumulated Depreciation 300
To book depreciation.

8. Your client who gave you the retainer calls you for an hour's work. You charge $100 and take it from the retainer.

7/1/xx

DR Client Deposit   100
    CR Bookkeeping Income   100
To book income earned.

9. You decide to take out a business owner's insurance policy, which will cover you from July 1 through June 30 of the following year. The $500 bill for the policy arrives via email and it's payable in 30 days.

7/1/xx

DR Prepaid Insurance   500
    CR Accounts Payable   500
To book insurance.

Your client pays you for three hours of bookkeeping, $300, by check and you deposit it.

7/1/xx

Dr Checking   300
    CR Bookkeeping Income 300
to book income earned and received.

Now, use this page to post your entries to your T-accounts.

Checking

2910	1500
300	
1710	

Legal Expense

300	

Accounts Payable

	300
	500
	800

Accounts Receivable

1000	

Clean Up Income

	1000

Credit Card Receivable

3000	3000
Ø	

Client Deposit

100	3000
	2910

CC Fee

90	

Credit Card Payable

	1250

Security Deposit

1250	

Laptop

1500	

Depreciation Expense

300	

Accumulated Depreciation

	300

Bookkeeping Income

	100
	300
	400

Prepaid Insurance

500	

Use this page to create your Income Statement from your T-accounts.

My Bookkeeping Business
Income Statement
For the Period July 1, 20xx

INCOME

Clean up Income 1000
Bookkeeping Income 400
Total Income 1400

EXPENSES

Legal expence (300)
Credit Card Processing Fee (90)
Depreciation Expense (300)
Total Expenses (690)

Net Profit 710

Use this page to create your Balance Sheet from your T-accounts.

My Bookkeeping Business
Balance Sheet
As of July 1, 20xx

ASSETS

Checking 1710
CC Rec.   0
Accts Rec. 1000
Prepaid Ins. 500
Laptop 1500
  Acc. Dep (300)
           Net 1200
Security Dep. 1250

Total Assets 5660

LIABILITIES

Accts. Payable 800
Credit card pay. 1250
Client Deposit 2900

Total Liabilities 4950

EQUITY

Net Profit   710
Total Equity   710

Total Liabilities
  + Equity 5660

Problem Set Eight – No More Training Wheels

To bring it all home, we will revisit your pet care business from Problem Set Four.

Create a journal entry for each transaction below. Assume all transactions happen on July 1, 20xx. Remember you need four things for a proper J/E.

1. You decide that in addition to selling your time for pet care services, you'll also sell pet products to your clients. As such, you know you need to bulk up your inventory, and in preparation for this you obtain a loan from your bank in the amount of $3000.

   7/1/xx

   DR Checking   3000
       CR Bank Loan 3000

   To book receipt of Bank loan.

2. Now it's time to buy that inventory. You place an order for $2500 worth of cat toys, dog toys, leashes, brushes – the works. You put this on your business credit card.

   7/1/xx

   DR Inventory   2500
       CR Credit Card Payable 2500
   To Book purchase of inventory.

3. Your new client has five dogs and wants a lot of dog-walking while she's at work. To get started, she agrees to give you a retainer for about one week of walks, or $250, via check, which you deposit into the bank.

   7/1/xx

   DR Checking 250
       CR Client Deposit 250
   To book receipt of client deposit.

4. You are out on a dog walk later that day, and a leash breaks! Quickly, you use a spare that you have in your bag. You had intended to sell this leash, so it was sitting in Inventory, but at this point you need to expense it as a Pet Care Expense for $5.

    7/1/xx

    DR Pet Care Expense 5
    CR Inventory 5
    To book usage of inventory.

5. You get a call from a cat owner who needs some grooming for his cat. While at the appointment, you not only charge the client for the grooming service ($45), but you also sell him a new de-matting brush for $10 and collect $1 in sales tax. The brush cost you $3. The client pays cash.

    7/1/xx

    DR Checking 56
        CR Pet Service Income 45
        CR Product Income 10
        CR Sales Tax Payable 1
    DR COGS 3
        CR Inventory 3
    To book income, sales tax, and COGS.

6. The client in item 3 calls you for an unscheduled dog walk, for which you take $30 out of her retainer.

    7/1/xx

    DR Client Deposit 30
        CR Pet Service Income 30
    To book income used from retainer.

7. Unfortunately, your commercial **doggie dryer** breaks! You call the pet supply store and order a new one for $400. They give it to you on store credit.

7/1/xx

DR Dryer 400
   CR Accounts Payable 400
To book purchase of asset on credit.

8. Suspend disbelief and assume you need to depreciate this doggie dryer. It has a useful life of 10 years and you'll use straight-line depreciation.

7/1/xx

DR Depreciation Expense 40
   CR Accumulated Dep. 40
To book depreciation expense.

9. You make a payment of $25 to your business credit card.

7/1/xx

DR Credit card payable 25
   CR Checking 25
To book payment on credit card.

10. While out on a dog walk, a prospect asks you about the collars on the dogs. Later that day, the prospect calls you to buy 10 collars for her dogs. Each collar retails for $28, and you collect that money in addition to $10 in sales tax. Each collar cost you $12, and you book COGS immediately.

7/1/xx

DR Checking   290
    CR Product Income   280
    CR Sales Tax Payable   10
DR COGS   120
    CR Inventory   120

To book sale of product, sales tax, and COGS.

Now, use this page to post your entries to your T-accounts.

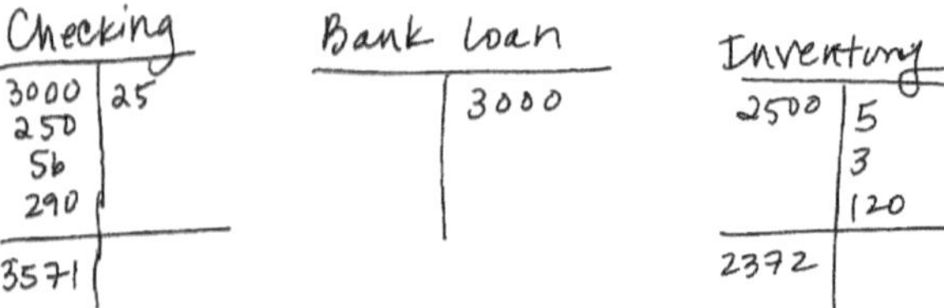

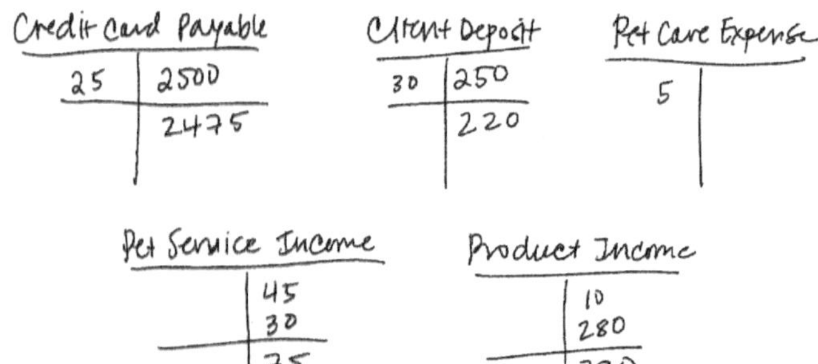

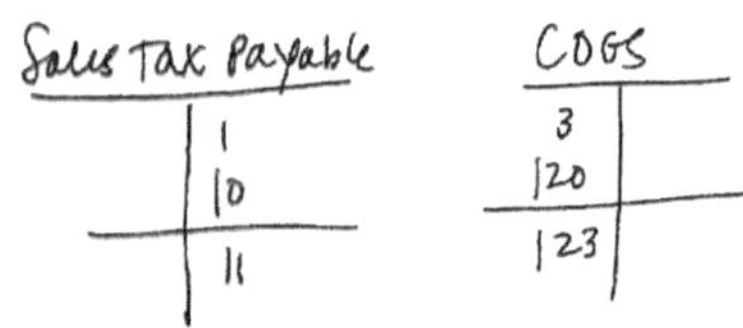

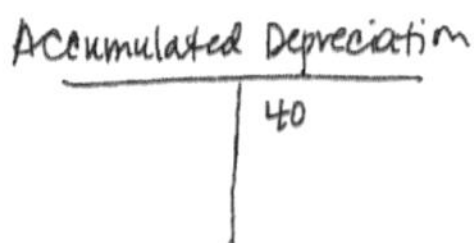

Use this page to create your Income Statement from your T-accounts.

My Pet Care Business
Income Statement
For The Period July 1, 20XX

INCOME
Pet Service Income   75
Product Income   290
        Total Income   365

COGS
        Cost of Goods Sold   (123)
        Gross Profit   242

EXPENSES
        Pet Care Expenses   (5)
        Depreciation Expense   (40)
                Total Expenses   (45)
NET PROFIT   197

Use this page to create your Balance Sheet from your T-accounts.

My Pet care Business
Balance Sheet
As of July 1, 20xx

ASSETS

Checking   3571
Inventory   2372
Dryer   400
   Acc. Dep (40)
      Net   360
Total Assets   6303

LIABILITIES

Accts Payable   400
CC Payable   2475
Sales Tax Pay.   11
Client Deposit   220
Bank Loan   3000
Total Liabilities   6106

EQUITY
Net Profit   197

Total Equity   197
Total Liabilities +
   Equity   6303